Acoustic Texture
Ceiling Stains

Use Kerosine to cut glass or
mirror It acts like a
coolant and makes a straight
cut on mirror

AFFORDABLE DECORATING

72 Projects & Ideas to Save You Money

The Home Decorating Institute®

Library of Congress Cataloging-in-Publication Data Affordable decorating / the Home Decorating Institute.
p. cm. — (Arts & crafts for home decorating) Includes index. ISBN 0-86573-376-7 (hc). — ISBN 0-86573-377-5 (sc) 1.
Handicraft. 2. House furnishings. 3. Textile fabrics in interior decoration. 4. Interior decoration accessories. 5. Interior
decoration — Amateurs' manuals. I. Home Decorating Institute (Minnetonka, Minn.) II. Series.
TT157.A34 1995 745—dc20 95-18911

CONTENTS

Affordable Decorating

Walls, Windows & Floors

Furniture

Accessories

AFFORDABLE DECORATING

Decorate your home at a reasonable cost and with great style.

As a do-it-yourselfer, you can give your home a new look without spending a lot of money. Make your own furnishings or adapt what you already have in a creative, fresh approach to home decorating.

Furniture can represent the largest portion of the budget. To save money, buy unfinished furniture in basic styles, enhancing the pieces with medallions, moldings, pierced tin panels, cutouts, or resist-stain stenciling. Consider substituting futons for the more expensive upholstered sofas and chairs, making your own futon covers. And sew slipcovers for director's chairs, to provide extra seating without a lot of expense. Create a table from PVC plastic pipe instead of buying an expensive high-tech table, or build a twig table with rustic, woodland appeal.

Floors and walls offer a creative opportunity with decorative painting, an inexpensive way to dramatically change a room. Paint a wood floor to achieve a high-end designer look. Or paint a sisal rug or a canvas floor cloth to create a customized area rug. For the walls, use a decorative painting technique, such as block printing or scumbling, instead of using an expensive wallcovering.

You can also save money by making your window treatments. For additional savings, select a style that uses a minimum of fabric, perhaps a Roman shade or a decorative roller shade. Complete the decorating scheme with accessories that look great, making accent pillows, framed botanicals, and rolled beeswax candles at a fraction of the cost of purchased ones.

DECORATING AT A SAVINGS

You can decorate your home at a substantial savings without sacrificing style and personalize your decorating scheme with customized pieces. Additional savings can be achieved by shopping for furnishings at discount stores or by purchasing knockoffs instead of name brands. In the comparison photographs here and on pages 8 and 9, the same great style is achieved, whether fine furnishings or budget-minded alternatives are selected.

OVER $6,000

Living room is decorated affordably, as shown below, with comfortable futon seating (page 85) that substitutes for an upholstered sofa. The bordered wool area rug in the room opposite adds rich texture; a similar texture is achieved with the bordered sisal rug (page 30). To imitate the look of the glass-top coffee table opposite, place a sheet of glass over an inexpensive planter (page 82) painted with a scumbled design (page 15). The draped window treatment opposite adds softness to the room; below, the center-draw Roman shade (page 48) falls in soft folds, but requires less fabric. Use pressed flowers from the garden to create your own framed botanicals (page 104), rather than buy expensive prints. Handmade decorative candles (page 107) add a finishing touch.

(Continued)

UNDER $2,500

DECORATING
AT A SAVINGS
(CONTINUED)

OVER $1,000

Kitchen dining area with checkerboard flooring has a striking look. Rather than use ceramic tiles, paint a wood floor (page 34), as shown in the affordable room below. As an alternative to dining chairs, make slipcovers for inexpensive director's chairs (page 88). For additional savings, add moldings (page 66) around the apron of a basic unfinished table; then paint and finish the wood yourself.

UNDER $500

OVER $1,200

UNDER $500

Contemporary setting *can be achieved affordably as shown at right. A coffee table made using PVC plastic pipe substitutes for an expensive high-tech table. Mock box pillows (page 123) and overdipped candles (page 107) you can make yourself replace costly purchased accessories.*

UNDER $150

OVER $550

Affordable finishing touches, *such as the rolled beeswax candles (page 107), decorative box (page 114), and other accessories at left, are alternatives to the more expensive items above. The scumbled wall design (page 15) substitutes for high-priced wallcovering.*

TIPS FOR DECORATING AFFORDABLY

Try a decorative painting technique, such as scumbling (page 15), to add interest to the room, instead of installing an expensive wallcovering. Paint is the least expensive way to change the impact of a room.

Sew a window treatment made with a minimum of fabric, such as a stitched-tuck Roman shade (page 41).

Slipcover a futon mattress with a hand-painted canvas to give it a designer look. Screen-print the fabric (page 24) to customize it, and sew the futon cover yourself (page 85).

Replace accessories for a fresh look. The decorative candles (page 107) and boxes (page 114) shown above add interest to a room without a lot of expense. Add texture to a room with rag rug pillows (page 119).

Restyle basic unfinished furniture by adding carved wood medallions, as shown at right, or with other decorative details (page 58). Detailing adds richness to furnishings and is often the sign of expensive furniture.

Rework what you already own, perhaps adding a painted border (page 30) to a plain sisal area rug as shown below.

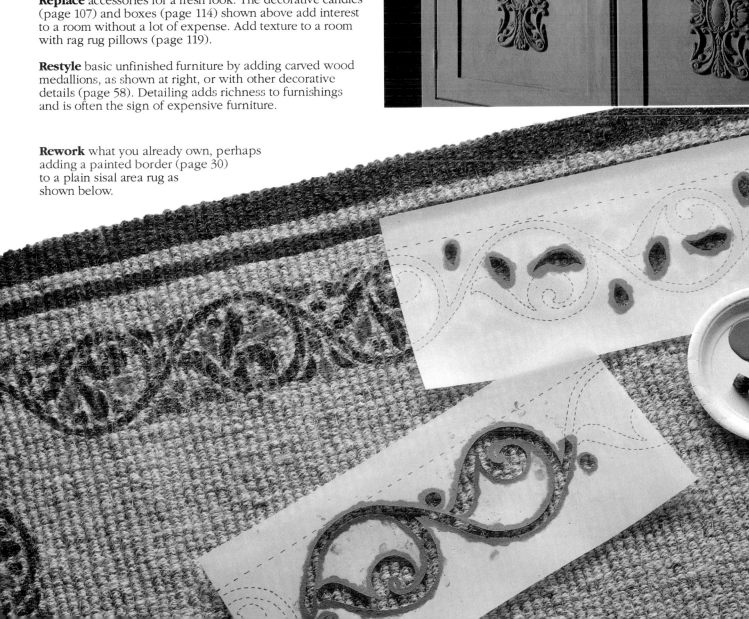

Walls,
Windows
& Floors

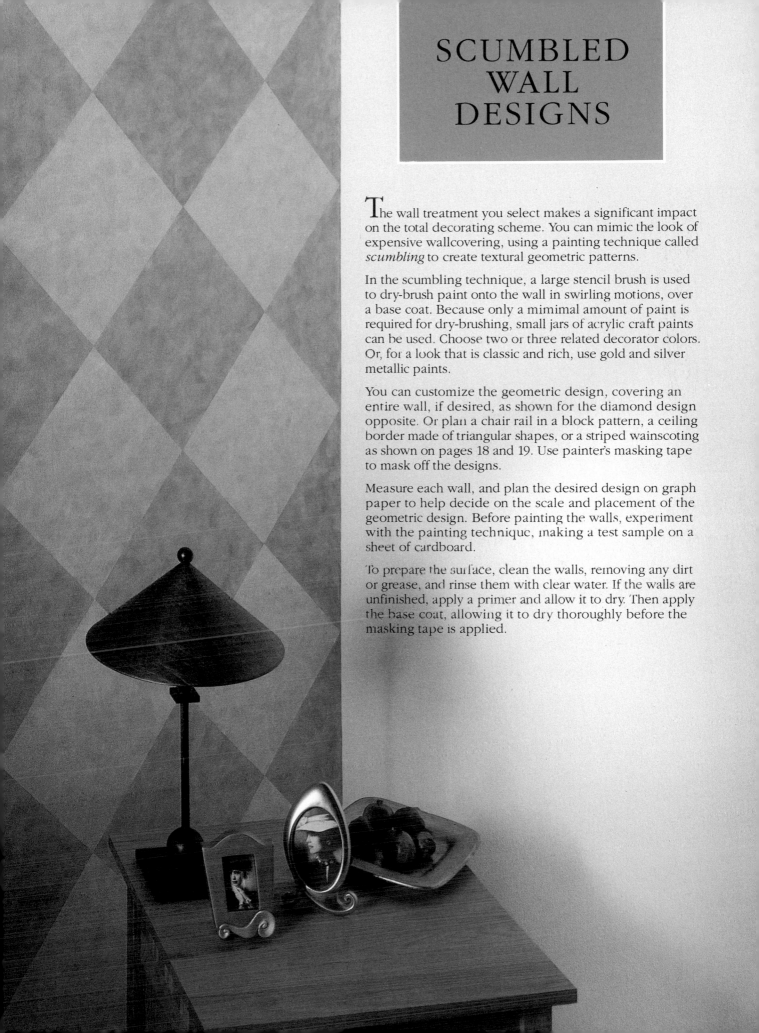

SCUMBLED WALL DESIGNS

The wall treatment you select makes a significant impact on the total decorating scheme. You can mimic the look of expensive wallcovering, using a painting technique called *scumbling* to create textural geometric patterns.

In the scumbling technique, a large stencil brush is used to dry-brush paint onto the wall in swirling motions, over a base coat. Because only a mimimal amount of paint is required for dry-brushing, small jars of acrylic craft paints can be used. Choose two or three related decorator colors. Or, for a look that is classic and rich, use gold and silver metallic paints.

You can customize the geometric design, covering an entire wall, if desired, as shown for the diamond design opposite. Or plan a chair rail in a block pattern, a ceiling border made of triangular shapes, or a striped wainscoting as shown on pages 18 and 19. Use painter's masking tape to mask off the designs.

Measure each wall, and plan the desired design on graph paper to help decide on the scale and placement of the geometric design. Before painting the walls, experiment with the painting technique, making a test sample on a sheet of cardboard.

To prepare the surface, clean the walls, removing any dirt or grease, and rinse them with clear water. If the walls are unfinished, apply a primer and allow it to dry. Then apply the base coat, allowing it to dry thoroughly before the masking tape is applied.

HOW TO PAINT A SCUMBLED WALL DESIGN

MATERIALS

- Painter's masking tape.
- Wide-blade putty knife.
- Carpenter's level; straightedge.
- Latex or craft acrylic paint, for base coat.

- Latex or craft acrylic paints in desired colors, for scumbling.
- Stencil brush, 1" (2.5 cm) in diameter.
- Disposable plate; paper towels.

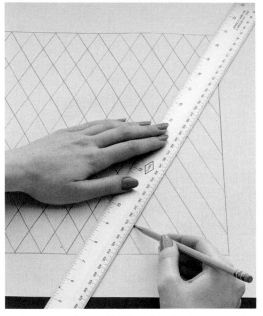

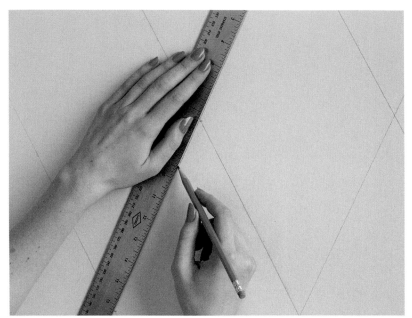

1 Measure the wall. Plan the design to scale on graph paper.

2 Apply base coat of paint, using paint roller; allow to dry thoroughly. Draw design on wall in light pencil markings, using carpenter's level and straightedge.

3 Indicate which areas are to be masked off, using small pieces of masking tape. Apply painter's masking tape to marked areas; use a putty knife to trim the masking tape diagonally at corners as shown. Press firmly along all edges of tape, using plastic credit card or your fingernail to seal tightly.

4 Pour a small amount of each paint color onto disposable plate. Dip the tip of the stencil brush into first color. Using a circular motion, blot brush onto folded paper towel until the bristles are almost dry.

5 Wrap fingers around handle of brush as if to make a fist. Brush paint onto the wall in vigorous, wide, circular motions, working in a small area at a time and changing the direction of the circular motions frequently; overlap the paint onto the masking tape. Build up the color to desired intensity, but allow base coat to show through. Use all of the paint on bristles.

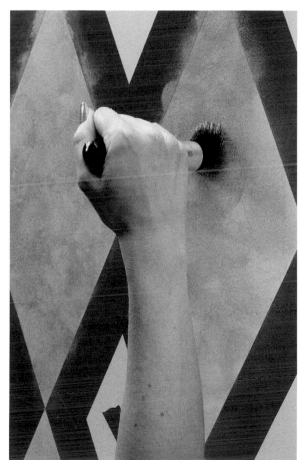

6 Dip the stencil brush into the second color; blot. Apply the paint randomly over the same area, building up color to varying intensities throughout the area. Repeat with a third color, if desired.

7 Repeat the technique to complete the entire wall, working in one small area at a time and blending areas together. Remove masking tape when paint is dry.

MORE IDEAS FOR SCUMBLED WALL DESIGNS

Wainscoting *features interrupted stripes, scumbled in greens and tans.*

Border design (above) is composed of triangular shapes. The designs are scumbled, alternating the colors from one triangle to the next.

Overall wall design (right) of diamonds within diamonds is created using wide masking tape.

Chair rail (below) in a block design adds simple detailing to painted walls.

BLOCK-PRINTED WALLS

Block printing is a simple stamping technique that can be used to apply repeated motifs to walls. In this technique, paint is applied to a printing block of wood and foam, then stamped onto the surface to be painted. The block prints can be aligned to form a border, arranged in a set pattern, or scattered randomly.

Closed-cell foam, available at art supply stores and hardware stores, works especially well for making printing blocks, because it cuts easily. Applied to a wood block for easier handling, the closed-cell foam has the necessary flexibility to make clean prints, even on somewhat irregular wall surfaces.

Closed-cell foam is manufactured in several forms. Thin foam sheets with pressure-sensitive backing can be purchased at art supply stores. These are easily cut with scissors into the desired shapes. Another closed-cell foam is neoprene, a synthetic rubber manufactured for use as an insulator. It is commonly available for use as weather stripping in a pressure-sensitive tape, 3/8" (1 cm) thick; however, in this form, the widest tape available is 3/4" (2 cm). Neoprene can also be purchased in sheet form, through suppliers listed in the Yellow Pages under Foam. A computer mouse pad made of neoprene can also be used, although the surface may be textured.

Use acrylic craft paints for block printing on walls. Make a stamp pad for transferring the paint to the printing block by soaking a piece of felt with the paint. A small amount of paint extender increases the open time of the paint, keeping the stamp pad moist longer. It is a good idea to practice with the printing block on paper before printing on the wall, to become familiar with the placement of the design in relation to the outer edge of the block.

MATERIALS

- Closed-cell foam, available as thin, pressure-sensitive sheets, pressure-sensitive tape, neoprene sheets, and computer mouse pads.
- Wood block, cut slightly larger than design.

- Acrylic craft paints; acrylic paint extender.
- Felt; sheet of glass or acrylic.
- Craft glue, if foam is not pressure-sensitive.

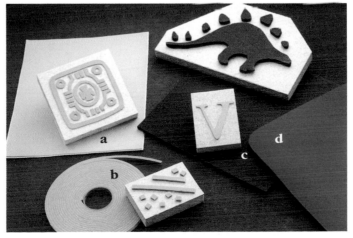

Printing blocks are made from closed-cell foam cut to the desired shapes and attached to a wood block. Closed-cell foam is available as thin, pressure-sensitive sheets **(a),** neoprene weather-stripping tape **(b),** neoprene sheets **(c),** and computer mouse pads **(d).**

HOW TO MAKE THE PRINTING BLOCK

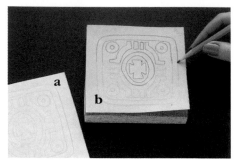

1 Cut tracing paper to same size as the wood block; make pattern for design on tracing paper. Mark top of design on pattern and on edge of block. Transfer design onto the back of the closed-cell foam **(a)**, using graphite paper. Transfer the mirror image of design on underside of wood block **(b)**.

2 Cut the foam on design lines, using scissors. Peel paper from pressure-sensitive backing; affix to the wood block, following the transferred design lines. If using foam without pressure-sensitive backing, affix foam to wood block with craft glue.

3 Glue the original pattern on opposite side of the block, taking care to position it in the same direction as the design on the underside.

HOW TO BLOCK-PRINT THE DESIGN ON A WALL

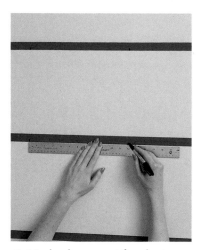

1 Mark placement for design motifs on wall, using masking tape or light pencil line.

2 Thin the paint slightly with an acrylic paint extender, about three to four parts paint to one part extender. Cut a piece of felt, larger than printing block; place felt pad on glass or acrylic sheet. Pour the paint mixture onto felt, allowing paint to saturate pad.

3 Press printing block into felt pad, coating surface of foam evenly with paint.

4 Press the printing block to the wall at placement mark, applying firm, even pressure to back of block. Remove the block by pulling it straight back from the wall.

5 Repeat steps 3 and 4 for each block print. Add paint to the felt pad as needed. Touch up any poor impressions, if desired, using a small brush, sponge, or piece of foam.

MORE IDEAS FOR BLOCK PRINTING

Block-printed border on this stitched-tuck Roman shade (page 41) matches the border on the wall. To block-print on the fabric, mix two parts of acrylic paint with one part of textile medium, rather than use an extender. In making the shade, omit the bottom row of rings so the printed border shows when the shade is raised.

Two-color border is created using a separate block for each color and section of the design.

Dinosaurs are block-printed randomly across the walls of a child's bedroom.

SCREEN-PRINTED FLOOR CLOTHS

A floor cloth with a custom screen-printed design makes a dramatic decorating statement at a low cost. For the screen printing, you may want to duplicate a design used elsewhere in the room, such as a fabric or wallcovering design, or use any design with a simple shape that can be cut out easily to make the screen.

An 18-oz. (500 g) or #8 canvas provides a durable surface for floor cloths and lies flat on the floor. It is available in widths up to 5 ft. (152.5 cm) at tent and awning stores and upholstery shops. After it is screen-printed, protect the floor cloth by sealing it with a clear acrylic finish. The sealed floor cloth may be cleaned by wiping it with a wet towel. If the floor cloth is used on a smooth floor surface, such as a wood floor, place a nonslip pad underneath it.

In screen printing, ink is forced through a fine screen onto the fabric. The sharp, clear, screen-printed designs are quick to produce. A special type of screen, constructed from stretcher bars and polyester mesh, is used for screen printing. A stencil, cut from Con-Tact® self-adhesive vinyl, is then placed on the screen; when the ink is applied to the screen, it passes through the open cutouts in the stencil. Use water-based textile inks that are transparent or opaque. After screen printing the fabric, heat-set the ink following the manufacturer's directions. It is important to practice screen printing on test fabric to become familiar with the technique and materials.

Screen printing may also be used on other projects in the room, such as futon covers (page 85), Roman shades (pages 41 and 48), roller shades (page 52), and mock box pillows (page 123), for a coordinated decorating scheme. If screen printing is used on projects other than floor cloths, the fabric may be laundered after the textile inks are heat-set.

MATERIALS

FOR CONSTRUCTING THE SCREEN

- Four stretcher bars, at least 5" (12.5 cm) longer than design.
- 14xx multifilament polyester mesh for most textile inks; 10xx multifilament polyester mesh for white and metallic inks.
- Masking tape; duct tape, 2" (5 cm) wide; heavy-duty stapler and ¼" (6 mm) staples.

FOR PRINTING THE FABRIC

- 18-oz. (500 g) or #8 canvas.
- Water-based textile inks that are transparent or opaque.
- Con-Tact self-adhesive vinyl.
- Mat knife; cutting mat; squeegee, ½" (1.3 cm) narrower than inside measurement of frame.
- Carpenter's square; straightedge.
- Plastic drop cloth; newsprint; paper towels; terry towel.
- Clear acrylic finish; synthetic-bristle paintbrush.

HOW TO MAKE A SCREEN-PRINTED FLOOR CLOTH

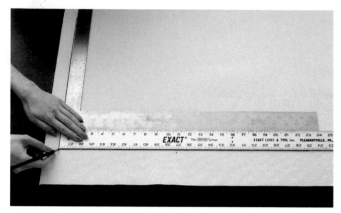

1 Mark canvas to desired size, using pencil, carpenter's square, and straightedge; mark lines in from selvages. Cut canvas. Press canvas so it lies flat.

2 Construct the screen, prepare the design, and screen-print the fabric as on pages 26 to 29.

3 Apply a clear acrylic finish, using a synthetic-bristle paintbrush; allow to dry several hours. Trim any loose threads at the edges of floor cloth. Apply two additional coats of clear acrylic finish, applying finish to the edges of canvas, to seal threads.

HOW TO CONSTRUCT A SCREEN FOR SCREEN PRINTING

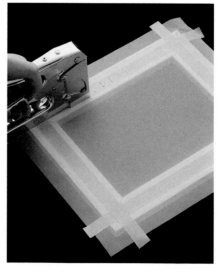

1 Assemble frame from stretcher bars, making sure the corners fit tightly and are squared. Cut the mesh 1" (2.5 cm) larger than the frame on all four sides; center the mesh over the frame, aligning the grainlines with the sides of the frame.

2 Apply masking tape to mesh, about ½" (1.3 cm) from outer edges of frame; smooth the tape, pressing from the center of each side to the corners. Staple mesh to frame on one side, through the masking tape, working from the center to corners; place the staples perpendicular to the edge of frame.

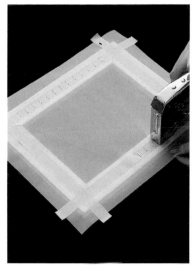

3 Staple mesh to opposite side of frame, pulling mesh tight. Repeat for the other two sides. Staple corners.

4 Trim the excess mesh. Apply duct tape over masking tape and staples, wrapping the tape around sides of frame.

5 Apply duct tape to upper side of screen to form a border, or trough, applying about ½" (1.3 cm) of the tape to mesh and remainder of tape to frame. Design must fit within taped area.

HOW TO PREPARE THE DESIGN FOR SCREEN PRINTING

1 Draw or photocopy the desired design; the design may be enlarged or reduced, using photocopy machine.

2 Hold the design up to a light source, such as a light table or window, and trace the design onto the paper backing of self-adhesive vinyl.

3 Cut the self-adhesive vinyl on design lines, using a mat knife.

(Continued)

HOW TO PREPARE THE DESIGN FOR SCREEN PRINTING (CONTINUED)

4 Remove paper backing carefully. Apply vinyl to underside of screen, overlapping duct tape border. Apply cutout details, if any.

5 Turn screen over, and press down firmly on the mesh; take care to secure cut edges of vinyl.

HOW TO SCREEN-PRINT THE FABRIC

1 Place a plastic drop cloth over the work area, including table and floor. Place a terry towel on table over the drop cloth; the padded surface helps to produce a better print. Place a sheet of newsprint over the towel. Place the fabric, right side up, over the newsprint. Position the screen over fabric.

2 Place about 2 T. to 3 T. (30 to 45 mL) of textile ink along the vinyl next to design area or along border. Applying firm, even pressure, use squeegee to pull the ink back and forth across the screen until the ink is evenly distributed. Too many repetitions cause the ink to soak through the fabric; too few cause an uneven or incomplete design.

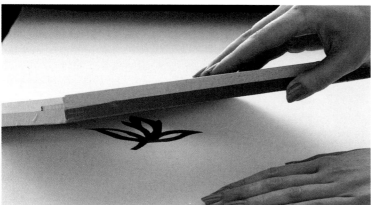

3 Lift screen slowly to a low angle, taking care that ink does not run onto fabric; carefully peel off fabric. Between prints, rest the screen so one edge is slightly elevated, and rest the squeegee on a stand or lid. Allow screen-printed fabric to dry before printing any nearby designs, to avoid placing screen over wet ink.

4 Set the screen-printed fabric aside to dry for 24 hours. Heat-set the ink by pressing the fabric with an iron for length of time recommended by the manufacturer; to heat-set ink on heavy canvas, press from the right side, using a press cloth.

HOW TO CLEAN THE SCREEN

Clogged screen. Wipe top of screen gently, using dry facial tissue, if print is uneven or incomplete.

Final cleanup. Remove vinyl from screen; wash screen as soon as printing is finished, using soft cloth. Wash off vinyl, and affix it to wax paper for reuse, if desired.

TROUBLESHOOTING PROBLEMS IN SCREEN PRINTING

Print is uneven or incomplete. Too much time may have been taken between prints, or ink may be too thick, causing clogged screen. Thin the ink, if necessary, following the manufacturer's instructions. Wipe clogged screen, above.

Ink runs into fabric along edges of design. Ink was thinned too much, or the vinyl was not pressed firmly to the screen at edges of the design.

Print has uneven patches of color. The ink was applied unevenly, or the squeegee was not pulled across the screen often enough.

Ink soaks into fabric. Too much ink was used, or the squeegee was pulled across the screen too many times.

DECORATING
SISAL RUGS

Sisal rugs are inexpensive and durable floor coverings with a classic look. As an alternative to either wool or synthetic area rugs, sisal rugs can work well with any decorating style. Customize a sisal rug with decorative painting, or apply a contrasting fabric border around the rug, repeating one of the fabrics used for other room furnishings.

The term *sisal* includes true sisal as well as similar plant fibers, such as coir, jute, rice, sea grass, and maize. True sisal, coir, and jute are coarse fibers and can be rough in texture. The fibers used to make rice, sea grass, and maize

rugs are smoother in texture and less abrasive to bare feet. All of the plant fibers can be woven into various patterns, including squares, diamonds, herringbones, and chevrons.

For painted designs, select a rug made from coarse fibers, because the paint adheres better to a porous surface. Use acrylic or latex paints, applying the paint with a stencil brush. Designs that are medium-to-large in scale work best, due to the rough texture of the rug. Mask off areas to be left unpainted, or use a stencil to paint design motifs.

For fabric borders, use a mediumweight to heavyweight fabric, such as canvas or duck, affixing the fabric to the rug with hot glue. The border may be any desired width, but a 3" to 5" (7.5 to 12.5 cm) finished width makes a striking framed edge without covering up too much of the sisal.

Before painting or applying a border to a sisal rug or placing furniture on it, unroll the floor covering and let the fibers relax at least 24 hours. Sisal can be placed directly on bare wood, vinyl flooring, or concrete, but you may want to place a nonslip pad under the rug for safety.

Sisal is a family of plant fibers that includes: (top row, left to right) true sisal, maize, and sea grass; (bottom row, left to right) rice, jute, and coir. All of these plant fibers can be woven into a variety of patterns.

HOW TO PAINT BORDERS OR STRIPES ON A SISAL RUG

MATERIALS

- Rug of porous plant fibers, such as true sisal, coir, or jute.
- Acrylic or latex paints.
- Painter's masking tape.
- Stencil brush.
- Aerosol clear acrylic sealer.

1 Mask off borders and stripes with painter's masking tape, pressing it firmly to the rug; follow woven rows in the rug whenever possible.

2 Apply paint, using a stencil brush in an up-and-down motion and working the paint into the fibers of the rug. Allow to dry.

3 Remove painter's masking tape. Apply aerosol clear acrylic sealer to painted area of rug.

HOW TO PAINT A STENCILED DESIGN ON A SISAL RUG

MATERIALS

- Rug of porous plant fibers, such as true sisal, coir, or jute.
- Acrylic or latex paints.
- Stencil plates; stencil brush.
- Painter's masking tape.
- Aerosol clear acrylic sealer.

1 Plan placement for design on entire rug before painting. It may be helpful to position photocopies of stencil plate on rug to visualize the design and plan the spacing.

2 Tape stencil plate to rug. Apply paint, using a stencil brush in an up-and-down motion and working the paint into the fibers of the rug. Allow to dry. Apply aerosol clear acrylic sealer to painted area of rug.

HOW TO APPLY A FABRIC BORDER TO A SISAL RUG

MATERIALS

- Plant-fiber rug.
- Mediumweight to heavyweight fabric.
- Hot glue gun and glue sticks.

1 Cut strips of the border fabric, with the cut width equal to twice the desired finished width of the border plus 1" (2.5 cm). Seam the strips together as necessary for a combined length equal to the perimeter of the rug plus 3" to 4" (7.5 to 10 cm). Press seams open.

2 Press seamed border strip in half lengthwise, wrong sides together. Press under ½" (1.3 cm) on both long edges of strip.

3 Wrap border strip over edge of the rug, beginning at one corner, so outer fold is centered on the edge; extend the end about 1" (2.5 cm) beyond the corner.

4 Fold under extended end of border strip as shown, encasing the outer edge of the rug; secure with hot glue.

5 Secure the border strip to top side of rug at the inner folded edge, applying glue 3" to 4" (7.5 to 10 cm) at a time; use an ample amount of glue. Press border strip firmly in place; work quickly before glue sets.

6 Fold the border strip diagonally at corner to form miter; glue in place. Continue gluing along the next side of the rug.

7 Fold the end of strip diagonally at the last corner to form miter; trim off excess fabric. Glue in place.

8 Turn rug over, and repeat steps 5 to 7 on the underside of the rug.

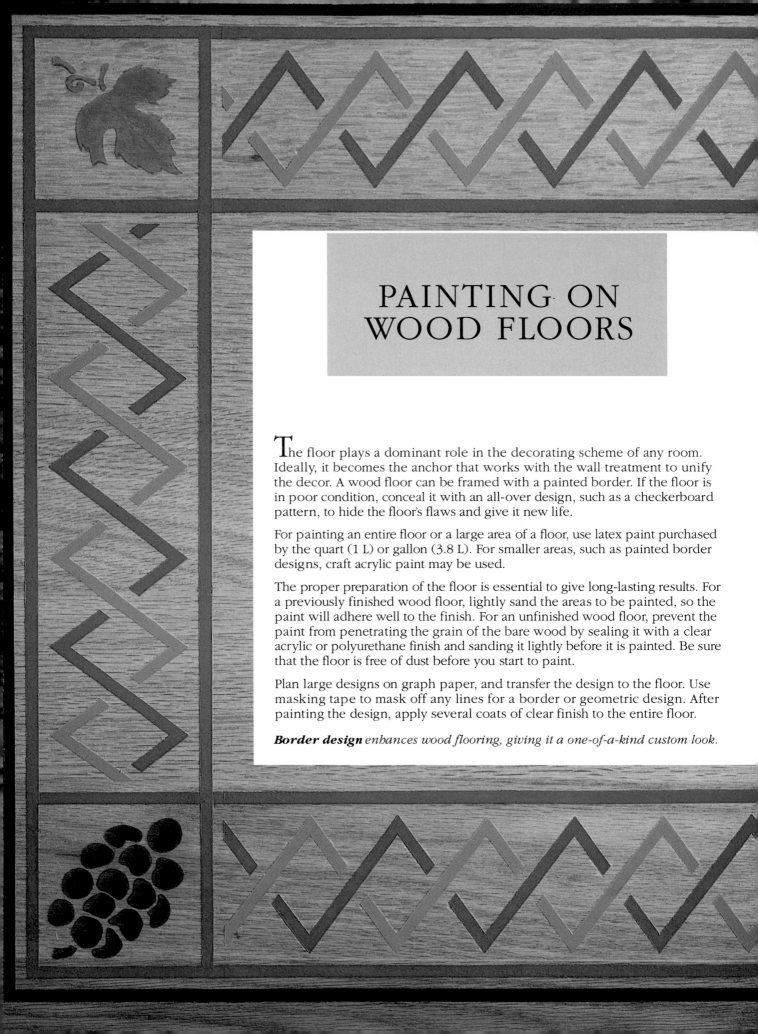

PAINTING ON WOOD FLOORS

The floor plays a dominant role in the decorating scheme of any room. Ideally, it becomes the anchor that works with the wall treatment to unify the decor. A wood floor can be framed with a painted border. If the floor is in poor condition, conceal it with an all-over design, such as a checkerboard pattern, to hide the floor's flaws and give it new life.

For painting an entire floor or a large area of a floor, use latex paint purchased by the quart (1 L) or gallon (3.8 L). For smaller areas, such as painted border designs, craft acrylic paint may be used.

The proper preparation of the floor is essential to give long-lasting results. For a previously finished wood floor, lightly sand the areas to be painted, so the paint will adhere well to the finish. For an unfinished wood floor, prevent the paint from penetrating the grain of the bare wood by sealing it with a clear acrylic or polyurethane finish and sanding it lightly before it is painted. Be sure that the floor is free of dust before you start to paint.

Plan large designs on graph paper, and transfer the design to the floor. Use masking tape to mask off any lines for a border or geometric design. After painting the design, apply several coats of clear finish to the entire floor.

Border design *enhances wood flooring, giving it a one-of-a-kind custom look.*

Checkerboard design has a classic look that works with any decorating scheme, depending on the colors selected.

MATERIALS

- Graph paper.
- Tape measure; straightedge.
- Fine sandpaper.
- Tack cloth.

- Painter's masking tape.
- Latex or acrylic paint.
- Paintbrushes.

- Materials listed on page 21, for block-printed border design.
- High-gloss and satin clear finishes, such as acrylic or polyurethane.

HOW TO PAINT AN ALL-OVER CHECKERBOARD DESIGN ON A WOOD FLOOR

1 Sand the surface of previously stained and sealed wood floor lightly, using fine sandpaper, to degloss the finish; this improves paint adhesion. Vacuum the entire floor, and wipe with tack cloth.

2 Mask off baseboards with painter's masking tape. Paint the entire floor with the lighter of the two paint colors. Allow to dry thoroughly.

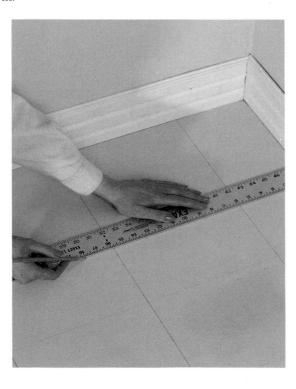

3 Measure the floor. Decide on the size of squares to be used. Plan the design so that areas of the floor with the highest visibility, such as the main entrance, have full squares; place partial squares along opposite walls. Mark design lines on the floor, using a straightedge and a pencil.

4 Mask off squares that are to remain light in color, using painter's masking tape, as on page 16, step 3.

5 Paint the remaining squares with the darker paint color. Remove the masking tape from squares carefully before paint is completely dry.

6 Apply a coat of high-gloss clear finish, using sponge applicator; allow to dry. Sand lightly with a fine sandpaper. Wipe with tack cloth. Apply two coats of satin clear finish.

HOW TO PAINT A STRIPED & BLOCK-PRINTED BORDER DESIGN ON A WOOD FLOOR

1 Sand the surface of previously stained and sealed wood floor lightly in the area to be painted, using fine sandpaper, to degloss the finish; this improves the paint adhesion. Vacuum entire floor, and wipe with tack cloth.

2 Mark design lines for border on floor. Mask off stripes in design, if any, using painter's masking tape; press firmly along edges with a plastic credit card or your fingernail, to prevent the paint from seeping under the tape.

3 Apply paint for the stripes, using a paintbrush. Remove masking tape. Allow paint to dry.

4 Block-print the designs as on pages 21 and 22. Seal entire floor with clear finish as in step 6, above.

MORE IDEAS FOR PAINTED FLOORS

Faux area rug, *painted on the floor area under a coffee table, becomes a whimsical accessory.*

Checkers game board *is painted on the wood floor in a corner of the family room. Mock box floor pillows (page 123) are used for comfortable seating while playing checkers.*

Stenciled design (above) is painted on a whitewashed wood floor, using precut stencils and a stencil brush.

Hopscotch is painted on a concrete game-room floor. To prepare the concrete floor, wash it with muriatic acid solution, following the manufacturer's instructions. Then paint it, using floor-and-deck enamel. It is not necessary to seal the floor-and-deck paint with a clear finish.

STITCHED-TUCK ROMAN SHADES

Stitched-tuck Roman shades have a neat, clean-lined appearance. They raise and lower easily, offering light control and privacy. They allow as much of the window to be exposed as desired and provide complete coverage when needed. And, because they require only a minimal amount of fabric, they are also an economical window treatment.

The shade has horizontal tucks stitched at evenly spaced intervals with alternate tucks stitched toward the front, then toward the back. When the shade is raised, the fabric folds along the tucks accordion-style. To help the shade hang smoothly, a weight bar is inserted into the hem at the lower edge. The depth of the lower hem is equal to the distance between the tucks.

This shade is attached to a mounting board and may be installed as either an outside mount or an inside mount. For an outside mount, the mounting board is installed above the window. For an inside mount, it is installed at the top of the window, inside the frame; the window frame must be deep enough to accommodate a 1 × 1 mounting board.

CALCULATING THE TUCKS & SPACES

You may choose the distance between the stitched tucks according to the look you want; a spacing of about 4" (10 cm) between the tucks is attractive. Before you cut the fabric, it is helpful to sketch the Roman shade as shown on page 42, indicating the number of tucks and spaces.

For an outside-mounted shade, if the estimated finished length of the shade is not evenly divisible by the desired space between the tucks, the measurement for the length can be rounded up until it is. For example, if you would like 4" (10 cm) spaces between the tucks and the estimated finished length is 45" (115 cm), you can round up the measurement to a 48" (122 cm) finished length, which is divisible by four. This allows for a 4" (10 cm) space between each of tucks, a 4" (10 cm) space at the top, and a 4" (10 cm) hem depth at the bottom of the shade, for a total of 12 spaces.

Sometimes the length of the shade cannot be adjusted, as for an inside-mounted shade that must fit within the window frame. In this case, the spacing between the tucks can be changed. For example, if the estimated space between the tucks is 4" (10 cm) and the desired finished length of the shade is 45" (115 cm), you may have ten 4½" (11.5 cm) spaces; this includes the spaces between the tucks, the space at the top of the shade, and the space for the hem depth at the bottom. Or you can have nine 5" (12.5 cm) spaces, including the top space and the hem depth.

When cutting the fabric and the lining, it is important to make square cuts so the finished shade will hang straight. Use a carpenter's square for accuracy in cutting.

INSTALLING THE SHADE

For a professional appearance, the mounting board is covered with fabric (page 46). On an outside mount, use fabric that matches the shade, because the covered board is visible on the sides.

For an outside-mounted shade, a 1 × 2 mounting board is used. Depending on whether you mount the board flat or on edge, it can be used for either a ¾" or 1½" (2 or 3.8 cm) projection, as shown on page 47.

For an outside mount with a 1½" (3.8 cm) projection, the mounting board is secured to the window frame or wall using angle irons. If you are securing the board to the wall, screw the angle irons into wall studs, whenever possible, using flat-head screws. If it is necessary to install angle irons between wall studs into drywall or plaster, use molly bolts or toggle bolts to ensure a secure installation.

For an outside mount with a ¾" (2 cm) projection, or for an inside mount, angle irons are not needed; the board is screwed directly into the window frame or wall (page 47). A 1 × 2 board is used for an outside mount, and a 1 × 1 board is used for an inside mount.

HOW A ROMAN SHADE WORKS

Back view shows the mechanics of a Roman shade. The shade is raised by pulling on the draw cord, causing the shade to fold in accordion pleats. The cords are strung through the rows of rings, then along the screw eyes in the mounting board at the top.

MAKING A SKETCH OF THE STITCHED-TUCK ROMAN SHADE

1 Draw sketch, indicating correct number of tucks and spaces. Label sketch with measurements of the finished length and spaces. Blue lines indicate back tucks, and red lines indicate front tucks.

2 Label the sketch with measurements for the finished width and the placement of the rings on the shade. The rings are positioned along the back tucks, starting 1" (2.5 cm) from the side edges and spacing remaining rows of rings evenly 8" to 12" (20.5 to 30.5 cm) apart across the width of the shade. The placement of the screw eyes on the mounting board is directly above the rings.

MATERIALS

- Decorator fabric.
- Lining fabric.
- Fusible web, ½" (1.3 cm) wide.
- ½" (1.3 cm) plastic rings.
- Shade cord; awning cleat.
- 1 × 2 mounting board for an outside mount or 1 × 1 board for an inside mount, cut to length as determined below.

- Screw eyes, number equal to the number of rings across width of shade.
- One ⅜" (1 cm) brass rod or weight bar, cut ½" (1.3 cm) shorter than shade width.
- Angle irons, 1½" (3.8 cm) long, and flat-head wood screws, for installing an outside-mounted shade.

- Molly bolts or toggle bolts, if installing angle irons for an outside-mounted shade into drywall or plaster rather than directly into wall studs.
- 8 × 1½" (3.8 cm) round-head screws, for installing an inside-mounted shade.
- Drill and drill bit; staple gun and staples.

CUTTING DIRECTIONS

Decide where the shade will be mounted. Determine the finished length of the shade from the top of the mounting board to either the sill or ½" (1.3 cm) below the bottom of the apron. Divide the desired space between the tucks into the finished length of the shade; if necessary, round the number up or down to the nearest whole number. This is the number of spaces, including the space at the top of the shade and the hem depth at the bottom.

Then divide the number of spaces into the finished length of the shade; this gives you the exact space between the tucks and the hem depth. There is one less tuck in the shade than there are spaces.

Determine the finished width of the shade. For an outside mount, the shade should extend at least 1" (2.5 cm) beyond the window frame on each side. For an inside mount, measure across the window, inside the frame. To allow for any variance in the width of the frame, measure it across the top, middle, and bottom. The finished width should be ⅛" (3 mm) less than the shortest of these three measurements.

Cut the fabric to the desired finished length of the shade plus twice the hem depth, plus ¾" (2 cm) for each tuck, plus the projection of the mounting board. Also add 2" (5 cm), to allow for any shrinkage in the length that

results from multiple rows of stitching; after the shade is sewn, any excess length is trimmed off at the top.

The cut width of the shade fabric is 3" (7.5 cm) wider than the finished width of the shade. If more than one fabric width is required for the shade, use one complete width for a center panel; seam equal partial widths on each side, matching the pattern in the fabric.

Cut the lining to the same length as the outer fabric minus twice the depth of the hem at the bottom. The cut width of the lining is equal to the finished width of the shade; if necessary, seam equal partial widths on each side of a center panel, as for the shade fabric.

For an inside-mounted shade, cut a 1 × 1 mounting board ½" (1.3 cm) shorter than the inside measurement of the window frame. This ensures that the mounting board will fit inside the frame after it is covered with fabric. For an outside-mounted shade, cut a 1 × 2 board to the desired finished width of the shade; this measurement should be at least 2" (5 cm) longer than the outside measurement of the window frame.

Cut the fabric to cover the mounting board, with the width of the fabric equal to the distance around the board plus 1" (2.5 cm) and the length of the fabric equal to the length of the board plus 3" (7.5 cm).

HOW TO MAKE A STITCHED-TUCK ROMAN SHADE

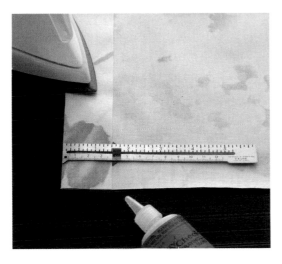

1 Seam fabric widths together, if necessary; cut fabric (opposite). Stabilize the side edges by applying liquid fray preventer, or finish the edges, using overlock or zigzag stitch. Press under 1½" (3.8 cm) on each side, for the hems.

2 Place shade fabric facedown on flat surface; place the lining on shade fabric, wrong sides together, with the upper edges matching. Place lining under side hems up to foldline.

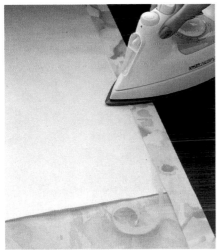

3 Fuse the side hems in place over the lining, using ½" (1.3 cm) strips of fusible web.

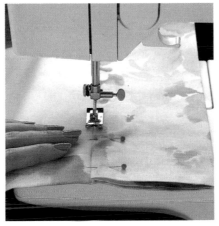

4 Press under an amount equal to the hem depth at lower edge of shade fabric; then press under again, to make double-fold hem. Pin in place. Stitch along upper fold.

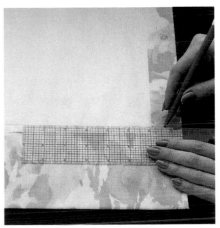

5 Place shade fabric facedown on flat surface. On the lining, mark a line for the first back tuck, ⅜" (1 cm) above stitched upper fold of hem.

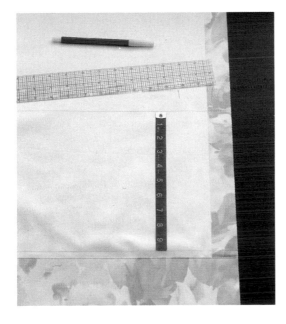

6 Mark lines on the lining for remaining back tucks; to determine distance between the marked lines, multiply calculated space between each front and back tuck by two, and add 1½" (3.8 cm). For example, mark the lines 9½" (24.3 cm) apart for a shade with 4" (10 cm) spaces between the front and back tucks. This allows for stitching the ⅜" (1 cm) tucks.

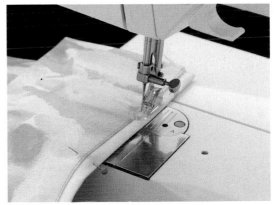

7 Pin lining to shade fabric along the marked lines. Press shade along first marked line, right sides together. Stitch ⅜" (1 cm) from fold, to stitch back tuck; repeat for remaining back tucks. For the first tuck, it may be helpful to use a zipper foot, because the stitching line is even with fold of hem.

(Continued)

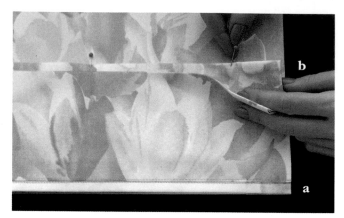

8 Fold shade, wrong sides together, aligning the first two back tucks **(a).** From the right side of the shade, press the fold for first front tuck **(b);** pin.

9 Fold and press the remaining front tucks. Stitch all front tucks ⅜" (1 cm) from folds.

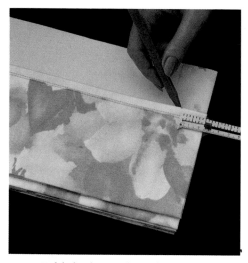

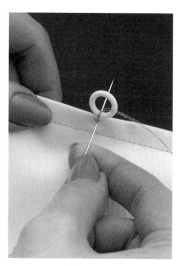

10 Fold shade, stacking front tucks and back tucks. Mark placement for rings on back tucks, beginning 1" (2.5 cm) from side edges and spacing remaining rows of rings evenly 8" to 12" (20.5 to 30.5 cm) apart across the width of the shade.

11 **Attaching the rings by machine.** Attach rings at marks, placing the fold under the presser foot with ring next to fold. Set zigzag stitch at widest setting; set stitch length at 0. Stitch over the ring, securing it with about eight stitches. Then stitch in place for two or three stitches, with stitch width and length set at 0; this secures threads.

11 **Attaching the rings by hand.** Tack rings by hand, using a double strand of thread, stitching in place through both fabric layers for four or five stitches.

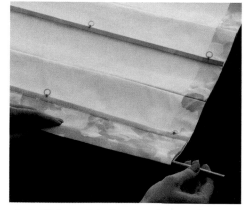

12 Slide weight bar into hem at lower edge of the shade. Stitch the side openings closed.

13 Cover the mounting board (page 46). Place the shade facedown on flat surface. Pulling the fabric taut, measure from the lower edge of the shade to the desired finished length; mark a line on lining fabric. This may change the upper space of the shade somewhat, but ensures that the shade is the correct length.

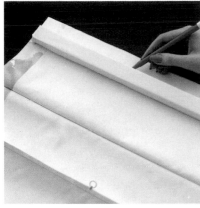

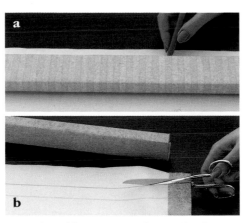

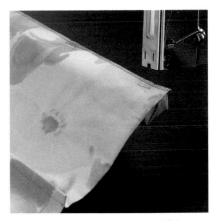

14 **Inside mount.** Place 1 × 1 mounting board on shade, aligning the edge of board with the marked line. Mark fabric along opposite edge of board, to mark the distance of projection away from first line. Cut on the second marked line.

14 **Outside mount.** Place a 1 × 2 mounting board on shade, aligning edge of board with marked line. For 1½" (3.8 cm) projection **(a)**, place board flat on table; for ¾" (2 cm) projection **(b)**, stand board on edge. Mark fabric and cut on the marked line as in step 14, left.

15 Finish upper edges of fabric and lining by stitching layers together, using overlock or zigzag stitch. Position upper front edge of mounting board along first marked line; finished edge of shade extends to back edge of board. Staple shade to top of board.

16 Install the screw eyes on underside of mounting board, aligning them with rows of rings.

17 Decide whether the draw cord will hang on the left or right side of shade. String the first row of shade, opposite the draw side. Run the cord through rings, from bottom to top and across the top through the screw eyes; extend the cord about three-fourths of the way down the outer edge of shade, for the draw cord.

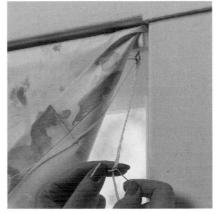

18 Cut and tie cord for first row securely at bottom ring. String the remaining rows, running cord through each succeeding row of rings and through screw eyes; cut and tie each cord at bottom ring. Apply fabric glue to knots, to prevent them from fraying or becoming untied.

19 Mount shade to wall or window frame (pages 46 and 47). Adjust length of cords, with shade lowered so the tension on each cord is equal. Tie cords together just below screw eye. Braid cords to the desired length. Knot end of braided cord.

20 Screw awning cleat into window frame or wall. When the shade is raised, wrap the cord around awning cleat.

HOW TO COVER THE MOUNTING BOARD

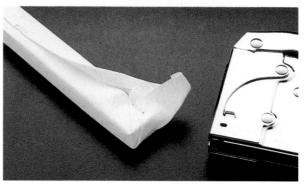

2 Miter fabric at corners on the side of board with unfolded fabric edge; finger-press. Staple miters in place near raw edge.

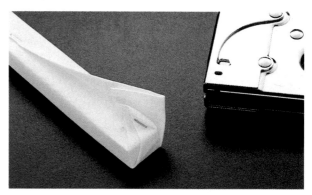

1 Cut mounting board and fabric (page 42). Center board on wrong side of fabric. Staple one long edge of fabric to the board, placing staples about 8" (20.5 cm) apart; do not staple within 6" (15 cm) of the ends. Wrap fabric around the board. Fold under ⅜" (1 cm) on long edge; staple to board, placing the staples about 6" (15 cm) apart.

3 Miter fabric at corners on the side of board with folded fabric edge; finger-press. Fold under the excess fabric at ends; staple near fold.

HOW TO INSTALL AN INSIDE-MOUNTED BOARD

1 Predrill screw holes through 1 × 1 board and into the window frame, using ⅛" (3.18 mm) drill bit and drilling from bottom of board; drill holes near each end of board and, for wide shades, in center.

2 Secure the board, using 8 × 1½" (3.8 cm) round-head screws.

HOW TO INSTALL AN OUTSIDE-MOUNTED BOARD

1 **For 1½" (3.8 cm) projection.** Mark screw holes for angle irons on the bottom of 1 × 2 board, positioning the angle irons outside the screw eyes, using 8 × ¾" (2 cm) flat-head screws. For wide shades, also mark for center-support angle irons, so the angle irons are spaced at 45" (115 cm) intervals or less.

2 Predrill screw holes into board; size of drill bit depends on screw size required for angle iron. Screw angle irons to board.

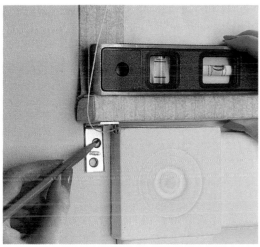

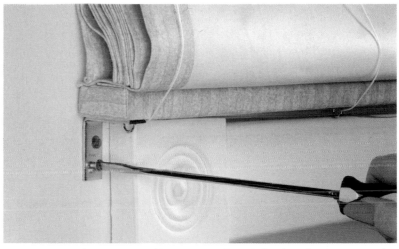

3 Hold board at desired placement, making sure it is level; mark screw holes on wall or window frame.

4 Secure angle irons to wall, using ¾" (2 cm) flat-head screws into the wall studs; if angle irons are not positioned at wall studs, use molly bolts or toggle bolts.

1 **For ¾" (2 cm) projection.** Predrill screw holes through 1 × 2 board and into the wall or window frame, using a ⅛" (3.18 mm) drill bit and drilling from front of board; drill holes near each end of board and, for wide shades, in the center. If not drilling into the window frame or wall studs, drill holes the correct size for molly or toggle bolts.

2 Secure board into the window frame or wall studs, using 8 × 1½" (3.8 cm) round-head screws. Or use molly or toggle bolts into drywall or plaster.

BANDED ROMAN SHADES
WITH A CENTER DRAW

A banded Roman shade that draws up the center requires only a minimal amount of fabric, but is a stylish treatment that provides privacy and light control. When raised, the shade gathers up the center, and the sides curve gracefully. Banding along the sides and lower edge adds interest to the shade.

Select a lightweight to mediumweight fabric that does not wrinkle easily, to create soft gathers when the shade is raised, yet maintain a wrinkle-free, smooth appearance when it is lowered.

Line the Roman shade, if desired, using lightweight to mediumweight lining fabric. For an unlined shade with a light, airy look, you may use a semisheer shade fabric, with opaque fabric for the banding.

MATERIALS

- Lightweight to mediumweight decorator fabric.
- Lining fabric, optional.
- ½" (1.3 cm) plastic rings.
- Two screw eyes.
- Shade cord; awning cleat; small drapery pull.
- 1 × 2 mounting board for an outside mount or 1 × 1 board for an inside mount, cut to length as determined on page 42.

- Angle irons, 1½" (3.8 cm) long, and flat-head wood screws, for installing an outside-mounted shade.
- Molly bolts or toggle bolts, if installing the angle irons for an outside-mounted shade into drywall or plaster rather than directly into wall studs.
- #8 × 1½" (3.8 cm) round-head screws, for installing an inside-mounted shade.
- Drill and drill bit; staple gun and staples.

CUTTING DIRECTIONS

Decide where the shade will be mounted. Determine the finished length of the shade from the top of the mounting board to either the sill or ½" (1.3 cm) below the bottom of the apron. Determine the finished width of the shade. For an outside mount, the shade should extend at least 1" (2.5 cm) beyond the window frame on each side. For an inside mount, measure across the window, inside the frame.

Cut the fabric to the finished length of the shade plus the projection of the mounting board plus ½" (1.3 cm). The cut width of the shade is equal to the finished width plus 1" (2.5 cm). If more than one width of the fabric is

required for the shade, use one complete width for the center panel; seam equal partial widths to each side of the center panel, to achieve the necessary width. If a lining is desired, cut the lining fabric to the same length and width as the outer fabric.

Cut the fabric strips for the banded edges, with the cut width of the strips 1" (2.5 cm) wider than the desired finished width of the band. For the side bands, cut two fabric strips equal to the cut length of the shade. For the lower band, cut one fabric strip equal to the cut width of the shade.

HOW TO MAKE A BANDED ROMAN SHADE
WITH A CENTER DRAW

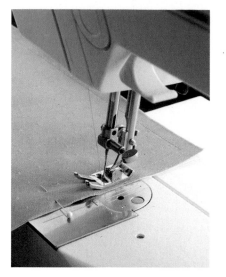

1 Seam fabric widths together, if necessary. For a lined shade, pin the lining to the outer fabric, wrong sides together, matching the raw edges; machine-baste ⅜" (1 cm) from raw edges.

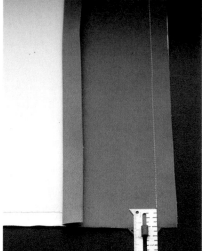

2 Press under ½" (1.3 cm) on one long edge of one side band. Pin band to the shade panel, with right side of the band to wrong side of the panel. Stitch a ½" (1.3 cm) seam, stopping ½" (1.3 cm) from the lower edge. Repeat for the band on the opposite side.

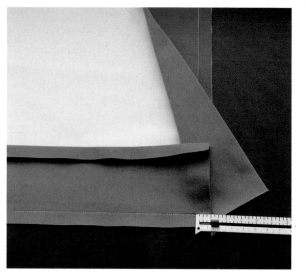

3 Press under ½" (1.3 cm) on one long edge of lower band. Pin to the lower edge of the shade, with right side of the band to wrong side of panel. Stitch a ½" (1.3 cm) seam, starting and stopping ½" (1.3 cm) from the side edges.

4 Mark band for mitering, placing pins at inner corner as shown.

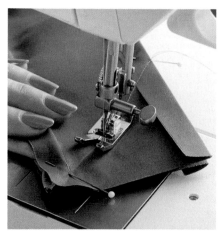

5 Stitch miters from the pin marks at inner corner to the end of stitching at outer corner; take care not to catch shade panel in stitching.

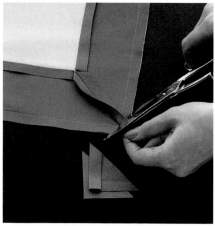

6 Trim mitered seams to ½" (1.3 cm), and press open. Trim the corners diagonally.

7 Press the seams open by pressing seam allowance of band toward band, using tip of iron.

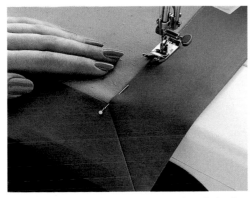

8 Turn the band to the right side of shade; press band, with seamline on the outer edge of the shade. Pin the band in place. Stitch around the band, close to inside fold. Finish upper edge of shade, using zigzag or overlock stitch.

9 Fold shade in half, right sides together. On the center fold, mark the placement for the rings, spaced evenly 4" to 6" (10 to 15 cm) apart; the ring at bottom of shade is to be positioned at stitching line on upper edge of the lower band, and the space above top ring should be equal to the other spaces plus the projection of the mounting board.

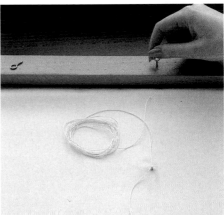

10 Hand-stitch rings in place with several small, vertical stitches; if shade is lined, catch outer fabric in stitching.

11 Cover mounting board (page 46). Staple shade to mounting board, aligning the upper edge of shade to the back edge of board. For a 1½" (3.8 cm) projection, place board flat on table; for a ¾" (2 cm) projection, stand the board on edge.

12 Install screw eye on underside of mounting board, aligned above the row of rings. Determine whether draw cord will hang on the right or left side of the shade; install a second screw eye ½" (1.3 cm) from the corresponding end of board.

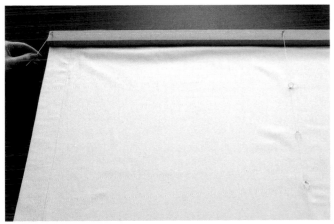

13 Place shade facedown on flat surface. Run the cord through the rings, from bottom to top, through the screw eyes; extend cord about three-fourths of the way down the outer edge of the shade. Cut and tie cord at the lower ring. Apply fabric glue to knot.

14 Mount the shade to wall or window frame (pages 46 and 47). Adjust the length of cord, if necessary; attach drapery pull to the end of cord. Screw awning cleat into the window frame or wall; when shade is raised, wrap the cord around awning cleat.

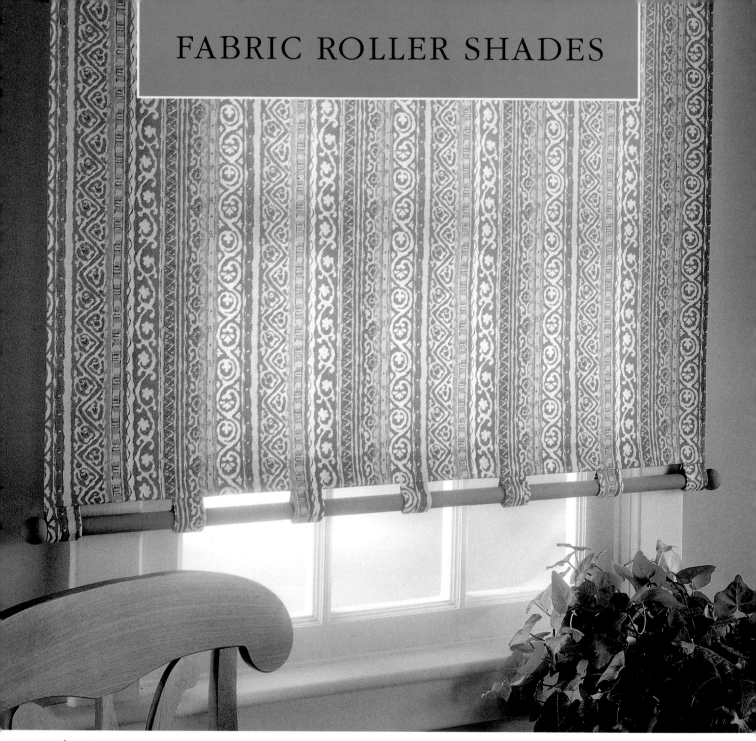

FABRIC ROLLER SHADES

A fabric roller shade is a very affordable window treatment, because it requires only enough fabric to cover the window and the hardware cost is minimal. For a basic roller shade, fuse a simple hem at the lower edge. Or, for a distinctive look, add tabs and a decorative rod with finials.

Pulley-system shades are easily raised and lowered to the desired height by pulling a cord on the side of the shade. These shades can be made from kits, complete with fusible shade backing that controls light and gives a uniform white appearance from the outside of the house. Depending on the brand of the kit, the shade fabric is attached either to an adjustable metal roller or to a cardboard roller that is cut to size.

For an inside-mounted shade, the window frame must be deep enough to accommodate the installed roller. If this is not the case, the shade can be installed as an outside mount, either to the front of the window frame or on the wall just beyond the frame. Install the brackets and mount the roller before cutting the fabric, to determine the exact finished width and length of the shade. Follow the manufacturer's instructions to determine the size of the roller and install the shade.

Avoid heavily glazed fabrics, such as chintz, because these fabrics do not bond well to the fusible backing. Also some fabrics with stain-resistant and water-repellent finishes may not bond well. Before using these fabrics, make a test sample to check the bond.

MATERIALS

- Pulley-system roller shade kit that includes fusible shade backing.

- Lightweight to mediumweight fabric.

- Fusible web, ⅜" (1 cm) wide, if not included in shade kit.

- Liquid fray preventer and small brush; masking tape or vinyl tape.

- ⅞" (2.2 cm) wooden dowel, for roller shade with a tabbed hem; finials, for outside-mounted shade with tabs, optional.

- Paint or stain and clear acrylic finish, for finishing the dowel and finials.

CUTTING DIRECTIONS

Install the mounting brackets and roller, and measure the roller as on page 54, step 1, to determine the finished width of the shade. Steam-press the fabric thoroughly to prevent shrinking. Using a T-square to ensure perfectly squared corners, cut the fabric 2" (5 cm) wider than the desired finished width of the shade and 12" (30.5 cm) longer than the desired finished length.

Cut the fusible backing 1" (2.5 cm) wider than the desired finished width of the shade and 12" (30.5 cm) longer than desired finished length, cutting perfectly squared corners.

TWO WAYS TO HANG A ROLLER SHADE

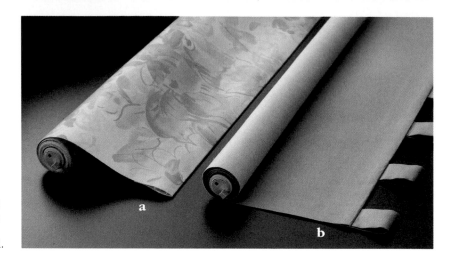

Determine how you will hang the roller shade before you begin. If the top of the shade will be visible when the shade is mounted, install the shade so it rolls off the front of the roller with the right side of the shade facing out as it wraps around the roller **(a).** If the roller will be concealed by a valance or cornice, the shade can be installed so it rolls off the back of the roller with the wrong side of the shade facing out as it wraps around the roller **(b);** this allows you to install the shade closer to the window for better energy efficiency and light control.

HOW TO MAKE A BASIC PULLEY-SYSTEM ROLLER SHADE

1 Install shade brackets, roller, pulley, and end plug at window according to the manufacturer's instructions. Measure the roller from inside edge of end plug to inside edge of pulley to determine finished width of the shade. Cut fabric and backing (page 53).

2 Fuse the backing to wrong side of fabric, centering it on the width of the fabric; fabric extends ½" (1.3 cm) beyond backing on each side. Use a press cloth, and follow manufacturer's instructions.

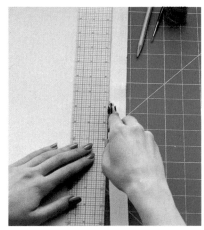

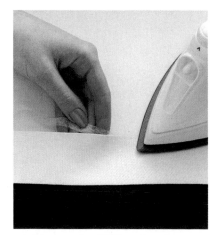

3 Mark finished width of shade on backing. Cut on marked lines. Apply liquid fray preventer to edges sparingly, using small brush.

4 Turn under 2" (5 cm) at lower edge, for hem pocket. Fuse in place at top of hem pocket, using fusible web.

5 Mark a line down the center of the roller by holding the roller firmly in place on a table; lay a marker flat on the table and slide it down the length of the roller.

6 Attach shade to roller by taping upper edge in place along marked line, from inner edge of pulley to inner edge of end plug. As shown opposite, tape shade to roller right side up if the shade will fall around front of the roller; tape shade to roller wrong side up if the shade will fall around the back of the roller.

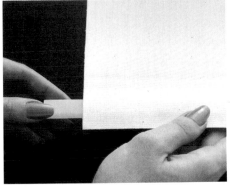

7 Trim hem stick to fit pocket at lower hem; slide into pocket. Mount roller shade into brackets.

HOW TO MAKE A ROLLER SHADE WITH A TABBED HEM

1 Cut desired number of tabs from fabric, 3" (7.5 cm) wide and 4½" (11.5 cm) long. Follow steps 1 to 3, opposite; cut 2" (5 cm) facing strip from lower edge of fused shade.

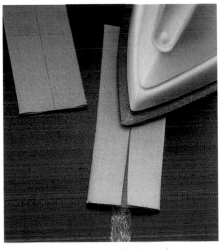

2 Fold long edges of tab to the center, wrong sides together; press. Fuse in place, using ⅜" (1 cm) strip of fusible web. Repeat for all tabs.

3 Fold the tabs in half; pin to the lower edge of shade on right side, with the outer edges of the end tabs even with the outer edge of shade and spacing tabs evenly. Baste in place.

4 Pin facing to lower edge of shade, right sides together, matching raw edges and hemmed ends. Stitch ⅜" (1 cm) seam through all layers. Turn facing to wrong side; fuse in place at upper edge and ends of facing, using fusible web.

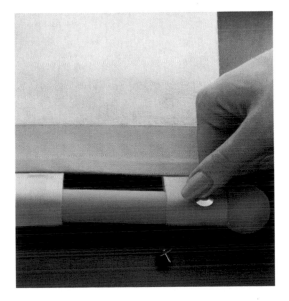

5 Cut dowel ⅛" (3 mm) shorter than finished width of the shade. Paint dowel and finials; or apply stain and clear finish. Insert the dowel into tabs. Attach finials. Secure with thumbtacks on back sides of the first and last tabs. Mount and install the roller shade as on page 54, steps 5 and 6.

Furniture

ENHANCING BASIC FURNITURE

For attractive, yet economical, furniture, purchase unfinished pieces, and paint or stain them yourself. Furniture in basic styles is the most reasonably priced and can be changed in various ways for the look of more expensive, detailed pieces.

Pierced tin panels can be added to door fronts for an authentic country look. Resist-stain stenciling creates the look of inlaid wood at a fraction of the cost, and wood medallions can be added to mimic traditional

Basic unfinished furniture can be changed in a number of ways, for the look of an expensive piece at a fraction of the cost.

wood carvings. Decorative wood moldings can add the finishing touch to furniture.

When shopping for unfinished furniture, look for good quality in construction. Choose wood that will accept the desired stain well. This may require some experimenting on scrap wood of the same type before making a final purchase. Sand the furniture completely and wipe the surface free of dust, using a tack cloth, before staining or painting the furniture piece.

Medallions (page 66) accent the doors and drawer of this painted armoire.

Pierced metal panels (page 62) are added to the recessed areas of these cabinet doors.

Decorative wood moldings (page 67) add subtle detailing at the top of this armoire and above the drawer.

Wood panel cutouts (page 68) add dimensional detailing to these cabinet doors.

Resist-stain stenciling (page 60) on this cabinet creates a contrasting design.

RESIST-STAIN STENCILING

Resist-stain stenciling is a technique that can be used on a piece of unfinished furniture to simulate inlaid wood. Stencil the design on the unfinished wood using aerosol clear acrylic sealer. When wood stain is applied to the furniture, the sealed stencil area will not accept the stain, producing a contrasting design in the natural wood tone.

Keep in mind that the wood grain will affect the finished appearance, because any variations in the wood will still be apparent after the stain is applied. For a distinct stencil design, use a clear wood with minimal grain markings.

If desired, the entire piece of furniture can be stained in a light shade before stenciling it, and stained a darker color after the clear acrylic finish is applied to the stenciled area. The stencil design is then the color of the first stain. This technique may be used to create several colors in the stencil, provided each succeeding stain color is darker than the previous one. Pretest the stains and stencil on a scrap of the same type of wood or on the underside of the furniture, to ensure good results.

When applying the aerosol clear acrylic sealer, use several light coats, rather than a few heavy coats, to prevent runs and to keep it from seeping under the stencil plate. Also, whenever possible, place the piece to be stenciled in a horizontal position.

MATERIALS

- Aerosol clear acrylic sealer.
- Precut stencil.
- Spray adhesive.

- Wood stain.
- Clear acrylic finish, optional.
- Newspaper; masking tape.

HOW TO APPLY A RESIST-STAIN STENCILED DESIGN

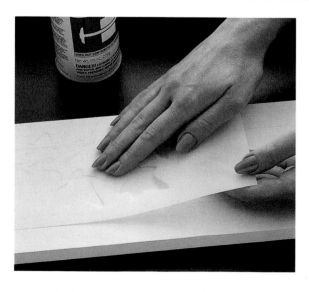

1 Apply spray adhesive to the back of precut stencil; allow to dry. Position stencil in the desired location on the unfinished furniture. Press firmly to ensure a tight bond, and cover the surrounding area, using newspaper and masking tape.

2 Apply five or six light coats of aerosol clear acrylic sealer to open areas of the stencil, allowing it to dry thoroughly between coats.

3 Remove the stencil plate. Remove traces of spray adhesive, if any, using lighter fluid. Stain the entire furniture piece; allow it to dry.

4 Apply aerosol clear acrylic sealer or clear finish to the entire furniture piece.

PIERCED METAL PANELS

Achieve an authentic country look by adding pierced metal panels to cabinet doors, trimming the panels with a narrow wood molding. On a flat-surfaced door, create a panel by mounting the pierced metal panel in the center of the door, edged with a wood molding. If the cabinet has recessed panels, mount the metal panels in the recessed area. Some cabinet doors have a removable center panel that can be replaced with the pierced metal panel.

For the pierced metal, purchase precut medium-gauge tin or copper sheets at craft stores in sizes ranging from 5" × 7" (12.5 × 18 cm) to 12" × 18" (30.5 × 46 cm). Other metals that can be used are thin-gauged galvanized sheet metal and hobby aluminum.

The necessary equipment for piercing the metal is minimal and inexpensive. Punching tools, awls, and engravers (shown opposite) can be purchased at craft stores in a choice of sizes. Although best results are achieved by using piercing tools, nails of various sizes and sharpened screwdrivers or chisels can be substituted.

Prepare the work surface by placing a piece of plywood over a cushion of newspaper, using a new piece of plywood for each panel that you pierce. To pierce the holes, strike the piercing tool with a mallet or hammer. Before beginning the project, experiment on a scrap of metal to determine how hard to hit the piercing tool in order to create the desired hole size, practicing the technique until you are able to pierce holes that are consistant in size.

You may purchase patterns for the pierced design. Or create your own pattern, using a simple line drawing or quilting stencil. Make a separate copy of the pattern for each panel you are piercing, saving the original. A new pattern is used for each panel so it is easy to see which holes have already been punched.

Piercing tools are available in several styles. Punching tools **(a),** used to punch copper and other lightweight metals, have sharpened points and slim wooden handles. Awls **(b),** used to punch holes in tin and other heavy metals, have sharpened metal points and knob-shaped wooden handles. Engravers **(c)** and chisels **(d)** have sharp chiseled ends for piercing short lines.

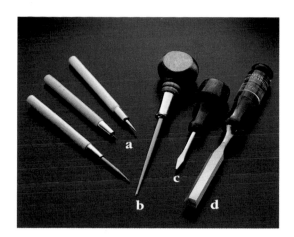

MATERIALS

• Medium-gauge tin or copper sheets, thin-gauge galvanized sheet metal, or hobby aluminum.

• Piercing tools or nails and sharpened screwdriver.

• Pattern and tracing paper.

• Scrap of plywood.

• Wide duct tape.

• Tin snips.

• Fine steel wool.

• Newspaper.

HOW TO MAKE PIERCED METAL PANELS

1 Cover the drawing with tracing paper; copy the lines, using dots and dashes to indicate holes and slits for pierced design. Use small dots for fine lines and large dots for bold lines. Unless the design indicates otherwise, mark evenly spaced dots.

2 Cut metal to correct size, using tin snips, as on page 64, step 1 for the flat-surfaced door or for the recessed-panel door. Remove fingerprints and smudges from the metal by rubbing it with fine steel wool.

3 Tape the metal panel along all edges to the plywood, using wide duct tape. Center the pattern on the metal panel; tape in place. Cushion the work surface under the plywood with several layers of newspaper.

4 Hold piercing tool at right angle to metal surface, resting the point of tool on a dot in the pattern. Strike with mallet or hammer, driving point of tool through metal.

5 Complete entire design, using tool with larger point on larger dots and tool with smaller point on smaller dots. Use chisel or engraver for the dashes. Remove the pattern slowly, checking to be sure that all holes and dashes are pierced.

6 Remove fingerprints and smudges with fine steel wool. If you want to prevent metal from aging, apply aerosol acrylic sealer. Or allow metal to age naturally.

HOW TO APPLY A PIERCED METAL PANEL
TO A FLAT-SURFACED DOOR

MATERIALS

- Prefinished door.
- Flat decorative wood molding.
- Wood glue.
- Masking tape.
- Small brads.
- Miter box and backsaw.

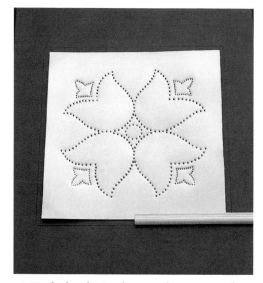

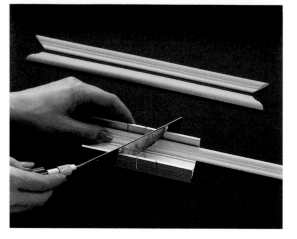

2 Measure and mark the length of upper and lower molding strips on outer edge; mark the angle of the cut. Cut the molding strips, using a miter box and backsaw. Check to see that the molding strips are exactly the same length. Repeat to cut side strips.

1 Mark the desired outer dimensions for molding frame on door, making sure corners are squared. Cut the metal panel with the length and width equal to these dimensions minus one width of molding in each direction. Pierce metal panel as on page 63, steps 1 to 6.

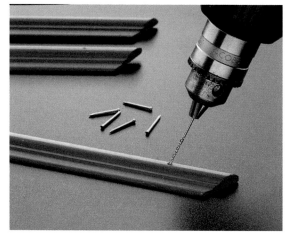

3 Paint or stain the moldings. Mark the placement of nail holes slightly toward the outer edge of the molding strips, 1½" (3.8 cm) from ends and at the center of each strip. Predrill nail holes, using drill bit slightly smaller than brads.

HOW TO APPLY A PIERCED METAL PANEL
TO A RECESSED-PANEL DOOR

MATERIALS

- Prefinished door.
- ¼" (6 mm) quarter-round wood molding or flat decorative molding.
- Miter box and backsaw.
- Wood glue.
- Small brads.

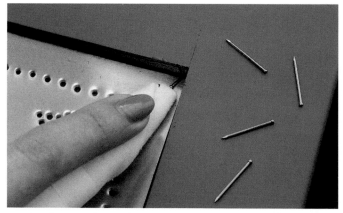

1 Cut the metal panel to exact measurements of recessed panel. Pierce metal as on page 63, steps 1 to 6. Secure the metal inside the recess with small brads inserted at an angle; to prevent scratching the metal, push brads in place using a screwdriver covered with cloth.

2 Cut quarter-round or decorative molding to fit inside the edge of the recess, using miter box to miter corners.

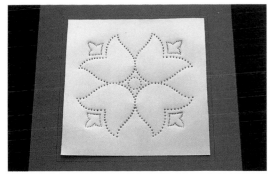

4 Center pierced metal panel on door along marked lines for frame. If door is not lying horizontally, secure metal panel temporarily with masking tape.

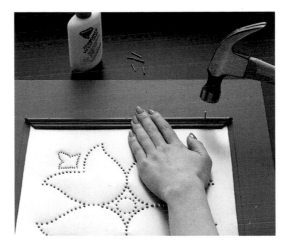

5 Apply wood glue sparingly to the back of the upper molding strip, toward the outer edge, using finger. Position molding strip on the door, aligning it with the markings and overlapping upper edge of the metal panel; secure with brads, leaving brads slightly raised.

6 Attach molding strips for sides of panel, applying glue to the back and placing brads at the upper corners only. Attach lower strip, making sure frame is square. Secure the remaining brads for the sides of frame.

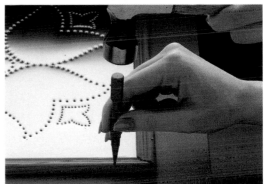

7 Countersink brads, using nail set. Touch up nail holes and mitered corners with paint, or fill them with putty to match stain.

3 Paint or stain the moldings. Mark the placement of nail holes slightly toward outer edge of molding strips, 1½" (3.8 cm) from ends and at center of each strip. Predrill nail holes, using drill bit slightly smaller than brads.

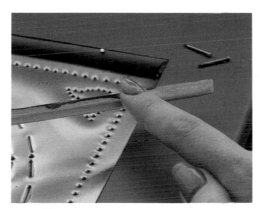

4 Apply wood glue sparingly to the back of molding strips, toward the outer edge, using finger. Position molding strips on door, around inner edge of recessed area; nail in place, leaving brads slightly raised.

5 Countersink brads, using a nail set. Touch up nail holes and mitered corners with paint, or fill them with putty to match the stain.

WOOD MEDALLIONS
& MOLDINGS

Embossed wood medallions and stock moldings can be added to plain, basic pieces of unfinished furniture. The medallions and moldings are reasonably priced and easy to apply.

In the instructions given at right, the medallions are stained to match the furniture. For contrasting medallions, stain the furniture in one color and the medallions in another color; then apply the medallions.

MATERIALS

- Unfinished furniture.
- Decorative medallions and moldings.
- Wood glue; wood filler.
- Small brads; nail set.
- Wood stain; clear acrylic finish.

HOW TO APPLY WOOD MEDALLIONS

1 Plan placement of medallion. Spread glue lightly on the back of the medallion; position on furniture.

2 Predrill holes for brads in recessed areas of the design. Secure medallion with brads; set, using a nail set. Stain the entire furniture piece; fill the holes with wood filler. Apply clear acrylic finish.

HOW TO ATTACH DECORATIVE MOLDINGS

1 Miter molding strip for one side of furniture piece at front corner, cutting a 45° angle; leave excess length on strip. Place back side of molding tight against back of miter box.

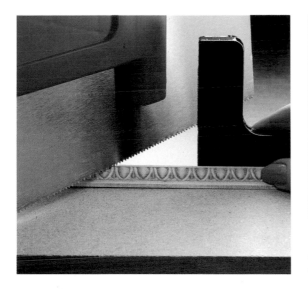

2 Repeat step 1 to miter front corner of the molding strip for opposite side of furniture, cutting angle in the opposite direction; leave excess length.

3 Position front molding strip against front of furniture piece. Mark the back side of molding strip even with outer edges of furniture, at both ends. Extend the mark slightly around the edges of molding.

4 Cut miter on the front molding strip from inner mark outward at 45° angle; cut ends in opposite directions. Angled cuts on the front molding will form mitered corners when aligned with side moldings from steps 1 and 2.

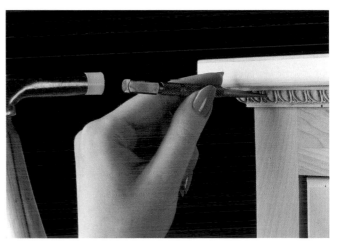

5 Position front and side molding strips on the furniture. Mark finished length of the side piece for a straight-cut end at the back corner of the furniture. Repeat for straight-cut end on the opposite side piece.

6 Cut both straight ends as marked on side pieces. Predrill holes and secure moldings to cornice, using brads; set brads, using nail set. Use glue to secure mitered ends of moldings. Stain entire furniture piece; fill nail holes with wood filler. Apply clear acrylic finish.

Cabinets and armoires can be customized with the use of cutout panels. Select a piece of unfinished furniture with door panels that are recessed on both the front and the back. A simple shape is cut from the door panel, using a jigsaw, and an insert panel made from ¼" (6 mm) plywood is inserted into the recess on the back of the door. For contrast, you may want to paint or stain the insert a different color than the door.

HOW TO MAKE WOOD PANEL CUTOUTS

MATERIALS

- Unfinished furniture.
- ¼" (6 mm) plywood.
- Graphite paper.
- Sandpaper.
- Wood glue; clamps.
- Jigsaw and fine-tooth blade.
- Drill and large drill bit.
- Paint or wood stain.
- Clear acrylic finish.

1 Remove the door. Transfer a simple design that will be easy to cut onto right side of door panel, using graphite paper.

2 Drill holes in several locations, just inside marked design lines, using a large drill bit.

3 Clamp door in place. Insert jigsaw blade into drilled hole; cut on design lines, stopping at any corners of design.

4 Sand edges of cutout. Paint or stain door as desired.

5 Cut panel insert from ¼" (6 mm) plywood to fit the recess on back of door. Paint or stain insert as desired.

6 Glue plywood insert to back of door; clamp until dry. Apply clear acrylic finish to entire door.

TWIG FURNITURE

Twig tables and ottomans have a rustic, natural look suitable for country or lodge-style decorating. In a contemporary setting, a piece of twig furniture can contrast with sleek furnishings. The only cost in building twig tables and twig ottoman bases is the price of the nails, making twig furniture a good choice for decorating on a budget.

For a twig table, the tabletop can be made by nailing a row of twigs to the upper frame. Or it can be made from weathered barn siding, pine planks, old wooden game boards, or glass. For a twig ottoman, sew a mock box pillow as on page 123.

Gather freshly cut twigs and branches as you walk in the woods or near a creek or river. Or visit a local brush recycling center. You may want to contact builders in your area to see if they will allow you to gather wood on property that is scheduled to be cleared of trees.

Many kinds of wood are suitable for building twig furniture. Often the shape and diameter of the branches and twigs that you find is more important than the variety of the tree. Twigs from different varieties can be used on the same piece of furniture, depending on the look you want.

Freshly cut wood is most desirable because it is easier to work with and, as the wood dries, it shrinks around the nails, resulting in sturdier construction. Look for sturdy branches that are reasonably straight and consistent in diameter to use for the table or ottoman legs. The twigs for the upper frame and the lower braces also need to be reasonably straight and consistent in diameter. The lower braces can be made from forked branches, if desired.

The size of the nails depends on the diameter of the twig being attached, because using a nail that is too large may cause a twig to split as it dries. Use 6d nails on twigs 1" (2.5 cm) or more in diameter, 4d nails on twigs ¾" to 1" (2 to 2.5 cm) in diameter, and smaller nails for twigs under ¾" (2 cm).

When constructing twig furniture, always predrill holes through the top twig and into the bottom twig. Use a drill bit slightly smaller than the diameter of the nail, such as a ³⁄₃₂" drill bit for 6d nails and a ⁵⁄₆₄" drill bit for 4d nails.

Twig tables and ottomans *have rustic appeal. The table shown opposite has a row of twigs as the tabletop. The ottoman at right is topped with a mock box pillow (page 123).*

MATERIALS

- Freshly cut twigs and branches.
- Galvanized flat-head nails in a variety of gauges, including 2d, 3d, 4d, and 6d.
- Twine.
- Pruners.
- Crosscut saw; hammer; drill and drill bits.
- Exterior wood sealer or clear acrylic finish.
- Fabric for mock box pillow, for twig ottoman.

HOW TO MAKE A TWIG TABLE

CUTTING DIRECTIONS

For the table legs, cut four reasonably straight twigs, 1½" to 2½" (3.8 to 6.5 cm) in diameter, with the length of the twigs equal to the finished height of the table minus the tabletop.

For the front and back of the upper frame and for the front and back lower braces, cut four reasonably straight twigs, 1" to 1¼" (2.5 to 3.2 cm) in diameter, with the length of the twigs equal to the finished length of the table.

For the sides of the upper frame and the side lower braces, cut four reasonably straight twigs, 1" to 1¼" (2.5 to 3.2 cm) in diameter, with the length of the twigs equal to the finished width of the table.

For a twig tabletop, cut straight twigs, ⅝" to ¾" (1.5 to 2 cm) in diameter, with the length of the twigs equal to the finished width of the table. To determine the number of twigs needed for the tabletop, divide the finished length of the tabletop by the diameter of the twigs.

For the diagonal braces, cut two twigs, ¾" to 1" (2 to 2.5 cm) in diameter, with the length of the twigs equal to the diagonal measurement of the finished tabletop.

If additional twigs are needed to support a large tabletop, cut the desired number of straight twigs to the same length as the front and back twigs of the upper frame; use twigs of the same diameter as for the upper frame.

1 Determine desired height, length, and width of table; cut the twigs (above). On the work surface, draw two parallel lines perpendicular to a horizontal base line, with the distance between lines equal to the length of the table.

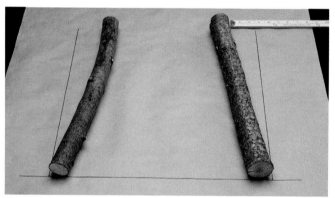

2 Place two table legs on work surface, with outer edges of lower ends at intersections of parallel lines and base line. Move upper ends of legs toward each other, so outer edges are 2½" (6.5 cm) away from the parallel lines.

3 Position the front twig of upper frame across and even with top of table legs. Center the upper frame twig on the legs horizontally.

4 Hold upper frame twig firmly in place, and predrill nail hole at one end, through the frame twig and into table leg; secure with nail.

5 Predrill nail hole at the opposite end of the upper frame twig; nail in place.

6 Position the front lower brace at desired distance from the lower ends of legs, centering it horizontally. Predrill the nail holes through the lower brace and into legs. Nail in place through the predrilled holes.

7 Repeat steps 2 to 6 for the remaining set of legs, attaching back twig of upper frame and back lower brace.

8 Mark a rectangle on work surface equal to length and width of finished tabletop. Stand the sets of legs up on the work surface, with outer edges of legs at corners of the rectangle. It is helpful to have an assistant hold the table sections in place as you proceed.

9 Center side twigs of upper frame just under front and back twigs of upper frame, extending the ends beyond legs the same distance as on front and back. Tie side twigs in place with twine.

10 Predrill and nail side frame twigs in place; after each nail, check to be sure twigs have not shifted and that lower ends of legs are still positioned as in step 8. Remove twine.

11 Position side lower braces just under front and back braces, extending the ends beyond legs the same distance as on front and back braces. Tie in place; predrill and nail the side lower braces to the legs. Remove twine.

12 Position the diagonal braces, crisscrossing them just above the front and back braces. Tie in place; predrill and nail to the table legs. Remove twine.

(Continued)

13 Position additional supports for tabletop, if desired, evenly spacing them between front and back twigs of upper frame.

14 Lay tabletop twigs across the upper frame, perpendicular to front, back, and support twigs; extend the twigs equally on front and back. Space twigs as desired, turning them as necessary for a flat surface.

15 Predrill and nail the tabletop twigs in place. Check occasionally to see that the tabletop twigs remain perpendicular to front and back.

16 Allow the table to cure for at least one month. Then apply exterior wood sealer or a clear acrylic finish.

HOW TO MAKE A TWIG OTTOMAN
WITH A MOCK BOX PILLOW

CUTTING DIRECTIONS

Determine the desired finished height of the ottoman; subtract the thickness of the mock box pillow (page 123) to determine the height of the twig base. Make the pillow, and, based on the size of the pillow, determine the desired length and width for the twig base of the ottoman.

For the legs, cut four reasonably straight twigs, 2" to 3" (5 to 7.5 cm) in diameter, with the length of the twigs equal to the desired height of the twig base.

For the front and back of the upper frame and the front and back lower braces, cut four reasonably straight twigs, 1" to 1¼" (2.5 to 3.2 cm) in diameter, with the length of the twigs equal to the finished length of the twig base.

For the sides of the upper frame and the side lower braces, cut four straight twigs, 1" to 1¼" (2.5 to 3.2 cm) in diameter, with the length of the twigs equal to the finished width of the twig base.

Cut twigs to be used as additional supports on the top of the ottoman, equal in diameter and length to the front and back twigs of the upper frame. The supports should be spaced about every 2½" to 3" (6.5 to 7.5 cm) across the top of the ottoman.

Cushion Size
16" x 22"

1 Make mock box pillow for the top of the ottoman as on pages 123 to 125; use purchased pillow form in the desired size of ottoman, or make your own form (page 120).

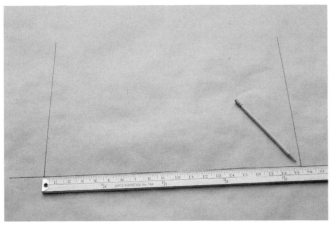

2 Determine the desired finished size of twig base for the ottoman; cut the twigs (opposite). On work surface, draw two parallel lines perpendicular to a horizontal base line, with the distance between lines 2½" (6.5 cm) shorter than length of twig base.

3 Lay two ottoman legs on work surface, with the outer edges along parallel lines and lower ends at base line. Position front twig of the upper frame across and even with the top of the legs. Center the upper frame twig on the legs horizontally.

4 Hold upper frame twig firmly in place, and predrill nail hole at one end, through frame twig and into leg; secure with nail. Repeat for opposite end of frame twig.

5 Repeat steps 3 and 4 for the remaining set of legs, attaching the back twig of upper frame. For each set of legs, position the lower brace across the legs, halfway between the upper frame and the lower end of legs, centering it horizontally. Predrill holes, and nail in place.

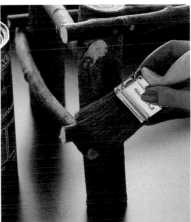

6 Mark a rectangle on the work surface 2½" (6.5 cm) shorter than the length and width of twig base. Stand the sets of legs up on work surface, with outer edges of the legs at corners of rectangle.

7 Continue building the twig base as on page 73, steps 9 to 11, and page 74, step 13. Reinforce point of attachment of upper frame twigs to the legs by predrilling and nailing a second nail at each end, at least ½" (1.3 cm) from first nail and at a slightly different angle.

8 Allow the twig base to cure for at least one month. Then apply exterior wood sealer or a clear acrylic finish.

MORE IDEAS FOR TWIG FURNITURE

Rag rug pillow (page 119) is used as the cushion on this rectangular ottoman. The rug is folded so the fringe falls along the front of the pillow.

Forked branches are used for the lower braces. Cut the forked branches longer than necessary; then recut them after their positions are determined.

Glass tabletop rests on this painted twig base. Round felt cushions are used to level the top and to pad the areas where twigs touch the glass.

Weathered barn siding, instead of twigs, is used for the tabletop below. The table is built as on pages 72 to 74, steps 1 to 13; then the table is turned upside down, and the top is attached. Insert screws through the front and back upper frame twigs and into the tabletop boards. A matte clear acrylic finish is applied to the entire table.

TABLES WITH PLASTIC PIPE BASES

For novelty coffee tables and side tables, PVC plastic pipe and joints can be used to create sturdy, inexpensive table bases. To complete the table, simply add a glass or plywood tabletop.

The PVC is available in a variety of sizes with inside diameters of 1" to 4" (2.5 to 10 cm). Elbows and crosses are available for joining the pipe sections together. PVC pipe is easily cut with a hacksaw, and any labeling by the manufacturer can be removed with sandpaper. The PVC can then be painted, if desired.

For the tabletop, you may use a circle or a rectangle of ¾" (2 cm) plywood, finishing the edge of the plywood with pressure-sensitive veneer edging. Or use a sheet of ⅜" (1 cm) glass for the tabletop. Precut circles of wood and glass are available in several sizes.

The instructions that follow are for the square side table and the rectangular coffee table shown here. For the side table, the base is positioned so the spokes serve as the top and bottom, with vertical supports; the base measures about 17" (43 cm) across and about 19" (48.5 cm) high.

A 20" to 24" (51 to 61 cm) precut circle of plywood or glass may be used for the tabletop.

For the rectangular coffee table, the base is turned so the spokes become the two ends of the base and the supports run horizontally along the top and bottom; the base measures 15" (38 cm) wide, 35" (89 cm) long, and 15" (38 cm) high. A precut 20" × 40" (51 × 102 cm) sheet of glass or a plywood rectangle may be used as the tabletop.

PVC pipe may be used to make the base for a side table or coffee table. The side table above has a plywood tabletop edged with matching veneer. The base of the glass-top coffee table at left is painted with an aerosol faux granite paint.

HOW TO MAKE A TABLE WITH A PLASTIC PIPE BASE

MATERIALS

- PVC plastic pipe with 1" (2.5 cm) inside diameter.
- Eight PVC elbows for 1" (2.5 cm) pipe.
- Two PVC crosses for 1" (2.5 cm) pipe.
- 20" to 24" (51 to 61 cm) round tabletop of glass or ¾" (2 cm) plywood, for side table.
- 20" × 40" (51 × 102 cm) glass or wood tabletop, for coffee table.
- Strap brackets to accommodate 1" (2.5 cm) pipe and wood screws, for attaching wood tabletop to PVC base.
- Wood filler, pressure-sensitive veneer edging with wood or metallic finish, mat knife, and brayer or wood block, for edging on wood tabletop.
- Acrylic discs, for cushioning glass tabletop.
- Medium-grit and fine-grit sandpaper; tack cloth.
- Hacksaw; rubber mallet.
- Latex or acrylic paint, optional, for table base; latex or acrylic paint or wood stain, for wood tabletop.
- Aerosol clear acrylic sealer or clear acrylic finish, optional.

CUTTING DIRECTIONS

For the side table, cut eight 6" (15 cm) lengths of pipe for the spokes of the table base; cut four 16" (40.5 cm) lengths of pipe for the vertical supports. For the coffee table, cut eight 8" (20.5 cm) lengths of pipe for the spokes of the table base; cut four 32" (81.5 cm) lengths of pipe for the horizontal supports.

1 Sand down any raised markings or labeling on PVC elbows and crosses, using medium-grit sandpaper. If you intend to paint the PVC, sand surface of all PVC pieces with fine sandpaper; this deglosses the surface so paint will adhere better. Wipe with tack cloth to remove any grit.

2 Insert a spoke into one opening of a cross; pound the spoke in as far as possible, using a rubber mallet. Repeat for remaining three spokes. Repeat for second cross and set of spokes.

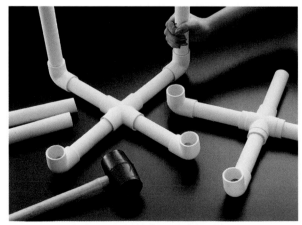

3 Slide elbows onto the ends of all spokes. Connect spokes by slipping supports into elbows. Pound the pipe into all openings as far as possible, using a rubber mallet.

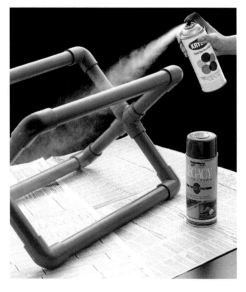

4 Apply aerosol paint to the table base or apply paint with a paintbrush, if desired. Allow to dry thoroughly. Apply aerosol clear acrylic sealer or a clear acrylic finish, if desired. Omit steps 5 to 9 if using a glass tabletop; cushion the glass tabletop from table base by placing acrylic discs under the glass.

5 Apply wood filler to the edge of plywood tabletop. Allow to dry.

6 Sand the edge of plywood tabletop until smooth, using fine-grit sandpaper; sand all surfaces of tabletop. Wipe with tack cloth.

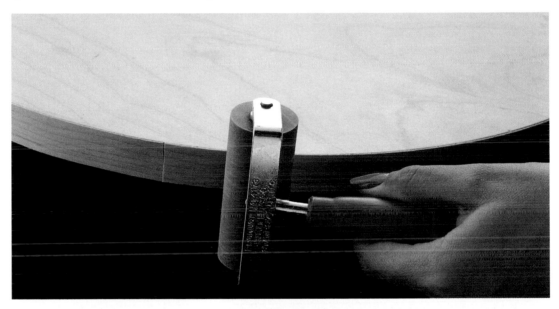

7 Peel protective film from back of pressure-sensitive veneer edging; apply to edge of plywood, aligning it to top of tabletop. Cut edging to butt ends. Press edging firmly in place, using brayer or wood block.

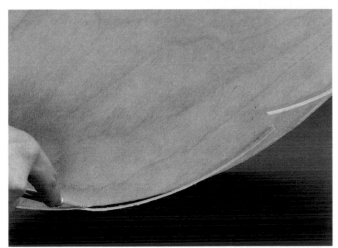

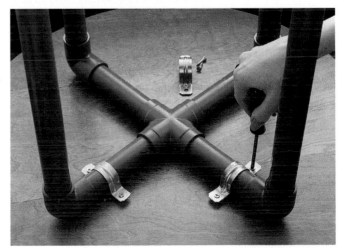

8 Trim excess edging on the underside, using mat knife, cutting from back of edging with tabletop standing on edge. Sand wood edging lightly. Paint or stain tabletop as desired. If metallic veneer tape is used, remove protective outer film.

9 Center the table base on the underside of the tabletop. Position 1" (2.5 cm) strap clamps; mark and predrill holes for the screws. Screw clamps in place.

MORE IDEAS
FOR TABLES

Wooden planter (right) provides a
sturdy base for a glass tabletop.

Picket fencing (below) in premade
36" (91.5 cm) sections is used for
the square coffee table in this country
room. Simply cut off the stakes at the
bottom of the fencing, join the sections
with corner braces, and paint the
table base.

Strawberry pots, *sponge-painted to match your decor, make an interesting base for a glass tabletop.*

Cement tubes, *used for forming concrete, are wrapped with rope to create this table base. Secure the rope with glue as you coil it around the tube, and glue the wooden tabletop in place. The three wrapped sections on the table above were cut from one 4-ft. (1.27 m) cement tube.*

FUTON COVERS

A futon is an affordable piece of multifunction furniture that can easily be converted from a chair or sofa to a bed by changing the position of the futon frame from an upright to a reclining position.

SELECTING THE FUTON

Futon mattresses are available in the same sizes as regular bed mattresses, from crib size to California king, and in various thicknesses and qualities. Consider how much the futon will be used when deciding which mattress to buy. If you intend to use the futon for daily seating or sleeping, it is likely to be less expensive in the long run to purchase the highest quality you can afford. The futon frames are available in wood or metal and in a wide variety of styles and colors. When selecting the frame, consider its durability, the quality of the folding mechanism, and the design.

SEWING THE FUTON COVER

A futon cover is not only decorative, but also protects the futon mattress from becoming stained or worn. You can sew your own futon cover that coordinates with the decorating scheme of the room. For an affordable cover without any seams, use bed sheets instead of decorator fabric. Select a solid-colored sheet or a patterned sheet with a nondirectional design; this allows you to turn the mattress regularly with the cover on, maintaining even wear on the cover as well as the mattress. You may want to use solid-colored sheets and add your own custom design, using screen printing (page 24), as shown opposite, or block printing (page 21). For durability, purchase 100 percent cotton sheets with a high thread count. Two sheets sized the same as the mattress provide enough fabric for the cover, including the front, back, and boxing strip; for example, two full-size sheets make a cover for a full-size mattress. Before you cut the pieces for the futon cover, remove the stitching from the hems. Then launder and press the sheets.

The position of the futon mattress on the frame varies with the style. A full-size futon mattress may sit on a sofa frame so the mattress folds in the center; one half serves as the seat of the sofa, while the other half serves as the sofa back. When converted to a bed, the arms of the sofa frame become the head and foot of the bed. In another style, a full-size mattress may rest on a loveseat frame so the mattress folds into thirds, with the upper third as the loveseat back and the lower third folded under the middle third, for a double thickness on the seat. Or, the upper third of the mattress may fall over the back of the frame. When converted, the sides of the loveseat remain the sides of the bed.

Make the cover so the length of the sheet, or the lengthwise grain, runs from the seat to the back, rather than from arm to arm, when the futon is used as a sofa or chair. If you choose to substitute a decorator fabric for the sheets, the seams will also run from the seat to the back.

For ease in inserting or removing the mattress, the cover is constructed with a zippered closing that extends along three sides. Custom-sized zippers are available from upholstery shops and many fabric stores, where the zipper tape is cut to the necessary length.

MATERIALS

- Cotton sheets, sized the same as the futon mattress.
- Zipper, with the length of the zipper tape equal to combined length of the top, bottom, and one side of mattress plus 1" (2.5 cm).

HOW TO SEW A FUTON COVER

CUTTING DIRECTIONS

As shown at right, determine the desired finished width of the boxing strip **(a),** equal to the thickness of the mattress; pin-mark on opposite sides of the mattress. Measure across the mattress, between pin marks, to determine the finished width of the futon cover **(b).** Repeat to determine finished length of the futon cover **(c).**

Cut the front and back pieces for the futon cover, with the length and width of the pieces 1" (2.5 cm) longer and wider than the finished width and length of the futon cover.

Cut one piece for the boxing strip, with the cut length 1" (2.5 cm) longer than the length of the futon cover; the cut width is 1" (2.5 cm) wider than the finished width of the boxing strip. Cut one zipper tab, 4" (10 cm) long, with the cut width of the tab equal to the cut width of the boxing strip.

For the zippered boxing on one long side of the cover, cut two zipper strips, with the length of the strips 1" (2.5 cm)

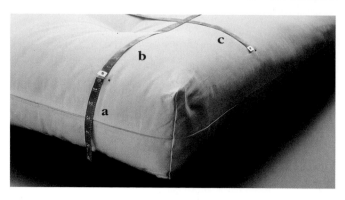

longer than the finished length of the mattress; the cut width of the zipper strips is 1¼" (2.5 cm) wider than one-half the finished width of the boxing strip. For the zippered boxing on the short sides of the cover, cut four zipper strips, with the length of the strips 1" (2.5 cm) longer than the finished width of the mattress; the cut width of the zipper strips is 1¼" (2.5 cm) wider than one-half the finished width of the boxing strip.

1 Stitch one short zipper strip to each end of one long zipper strip in ½" (1.3 cm) seams, right sides together; start stitching at the raw edge and stop ½" (1.3 cm) from the opposite raw edge. Finish seams, using overlock or zigzag stitch; press open. Repeat, using remaining short and long zipper strips.

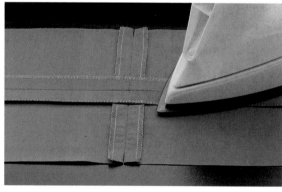

2 Place the zipper strips right sides together, matching the raw edges and seams. Machine-baste ¾" (2 cm) from the long edge where stitching of the end seams extends to the raw edge. Finish seams; press open.

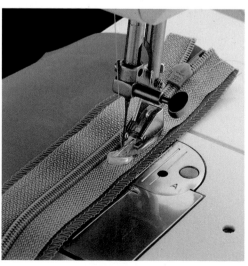

3 Fold the strip in half, right sides together, with one seam allowance extending. Place the closed zipper facedown over seam allowances, with the teeth centered on the seamline and ends of the zipper tape even with ends of strip. Machine-baste zipper tape to the extended seam allowance.

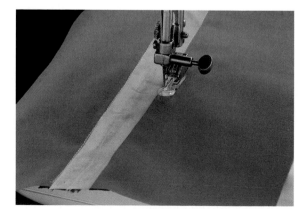

4 Unfold strip. On right side, center a strip of ¾" (2 cm) transparent tape over seamline. Stitch on both sides of tape, securing the zipper. Remove tape and basting stitches.

5 Press the zipper tab in half, with wrong sides together. Open the zipper about 2" (5 cm). At the top end of zipper, place the tab over the zipper strip, right sides up; stitch across the end, a scant ½" (1.3 cm) from the raw edges, stitching carefully over the zipper teeth.

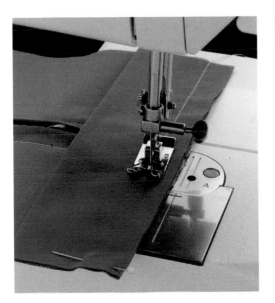

6 Stitch ends of the boxing strip to ends of the zipper strip, right sides together, stitching ½" (1.3 cm) seams; start and stop ½" (1.3 cm) from raw edges. Finish seams; press open.

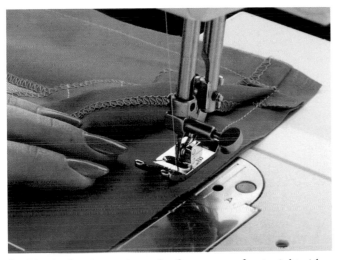

7 Pin the boxing strip to the futon cover front, right sides together, matching seams to corners. With boxing strip faceup, stitch ½" (1.3 cm) seam, pivoting at corners.

8 Pin the opposite side of boxing strip to the futon cover back, right sides together, matching seams to corners; stitch. Finish remaining seams.

9 Open the zipper; turn the futon cover right side out. Insert the futon mattress; close the zipper, hiding the zipper pull under the tab.

Simple slipcovers can be made for inexpensive director's chairs, transforming them into stylish seating. A mock box pillow made to fit the seat of the chair adds comfort. Create a pattern for the slipcover by pin-fitting pieces of muslin or old sheets over the chair frame.

One slipcover and pillow can be made from 3½ yd. (3.2 m) of 54" (137 cm) decorator fabric. For a custom look, block-print (page 20) or screen-print (page 24) a design on plain fabric. Designer sheets may also be used; usually one twin-size sheet is large enough to cut the pieces for one slipcover and pillow.

MATERIALS

- 3 yd. to 4 yd. (2.75 to 3.7 m) muslin, 54" (137 cm) wide, or old sheets, for pin-fitting the pattern.
- 3½ yd. (3.2 m) decorator fabric, 54" (137 cm) wide, for each slipcover, or one twin-size flat sheet.
- Polyester upholstery batting and polyester fiberfill.

CUTTING DIRECTIONS FOR THE MUSLIN PATTERN

Measure the distance from the floor up the back of the chair to the highest point. From the muslin or sheet, cut one back piece to the measured distance plus 4" (10 cm); the cut width is equal to the widest part of the chair plus 6" (15 cm).

Measure the continuous distance from the highest point down the inner back to the seat, from back to front of the seat, then down to the floor; from the muslin or sheet, cut one front piece with the cut length equal to the measured distance plus 4" (10 cm); the cut width of the muslin is equal to the widest part of the chair plus 6" (15 cm).

Measure the continuous distance at the side of the chair from the floor, up and over the arm, then down to the seat. From the muslin or sheet, cut one side piece with the cut length equal to the measured distance plus 6" (15 cm); the cut width is equal to the measurement of the chair from front to back plus 6" (15 cm).

Director's chairs (opposite) can be slipcovered to give them a new look. Any basic director's chair frame, such as the one shown below, may be used.

HOW TO MAKE THE PATTERN
FOR A DIRECTOR'S CHAIR SLIPCOVER

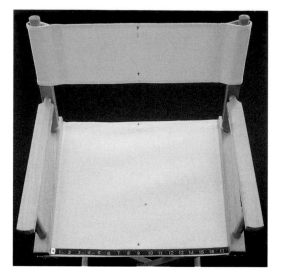

1 Pin-mark the center of chair back and seat. Mark a line down center of length of the patterns for the back and front seat. Pin pieces together, ½".(1.3 cm) from the upper edge. Mark seamline.

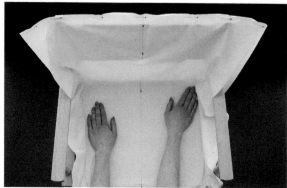

2 Pin the fabric to inner back and seat of chair, matching centers, with fabric extending onto floor; position seamline so it falls between back edges of back posts. Smooth fabric over the seat from back to front, allowing slight ease for sitting.

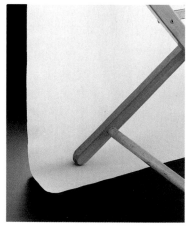

3 Allow back pattern to hang freely to floor. Place excess fabric under back legs of chair, keeping grainline straight.

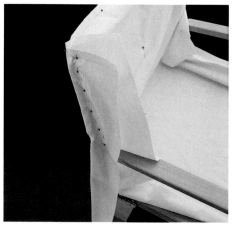

4 Wrap back pattern piece around one side of chair, meeting front pattern piece along the front outer edge of the back post. Pin back to front across top of post and along outer edge of post to arm.

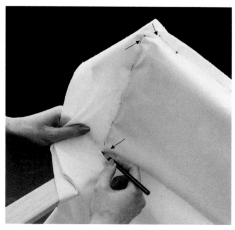

5 Mark dots on both pieces at back top of post, at front top of post, and at point where post intersects outer edge of arm (arrows). Mark seamline along pins. Trim excess fabric to within 1" (2.5 cm) of marked seamline.

6 Mark the seamline on the back pattern piece from dot at intersection of post and arm to the floor, using a straightedge; keep the line parallel to the raw edge and perpendicular to the floor.

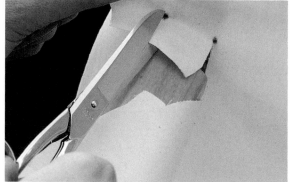

7 Mark a dot on the front pattern piece at point where post intersects inner edge of arm. Trim the fabric to within 1" (2.5 cm) of seamline, and clip to dots.

8 Smooth the front pattern piece over the chair seat. Mark seamline along the crease where seat meets the lower arm. Mark dots on the seamline at front and back of the seat. Trim excess fabric at the side of seat to within 1" (2.5 cm) of seamline; clip to the front dot.

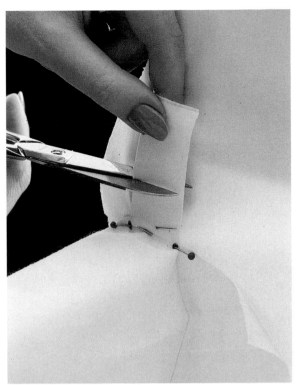

9 Mark a line on the side pattern piece, 2½" (6.5 cm) from the back edge and parallel to the grainline; pin to seamline of back pattern, as marked in step 6, allowing about 3" (7.5 cm) to extend onto the floor. Mark a dot at intersection of the outer arm and post; clip to dot. Trim excess fabric to within 1" (2.5 cm) of seamline, from top of arm to floor.

10 Wrap the side pattern over the arm and down onto the seat, keeping grainline of the pattern perpendicular to the floor on outside of chair. Mark a dot on the side pattern at inner arm where it intersects back post; clip to dot. Pin side and front pattern pieces together, matching dots. Trim excess fabric to within 1" (2.5 cm) of seamline between dots.

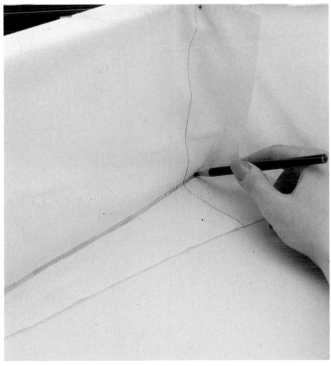

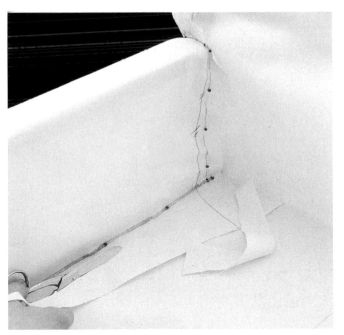

11 Mark seamline of side pattern along the crease where seat meets the lower arm. Mark dots on the seamline at front and back of seat.

12 Pin the side pattern to seat of the front pattern along marked seamline, matching the dots. Pin patterns together from dots at upper arm to dots at back seat; pins may not follow the previously marked grainline. Mark the seamline. Trim excess fabric to within 1" (2.5 cm) of pinned seamlines. Clip to dots as necessary.

(Continued)

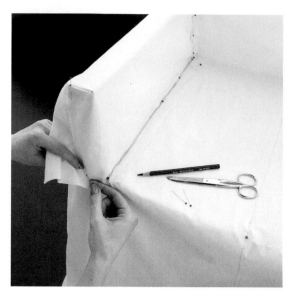

13 Clip to the inner front dot at lower arm. Wrap inner side pattern piece across the arm front to meet the outer side. Mark inner and outer front dots at the upper arm, and outer front dot at the lower arm. Pin together, matching dots; mark the seamline. Trim excess fabric, and clip to dots as necessary.

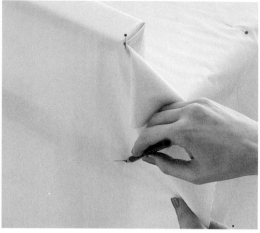

14 Insert pin through matched outer front dots at the lower arm, pinning through to side of slipcover. Mark dot.

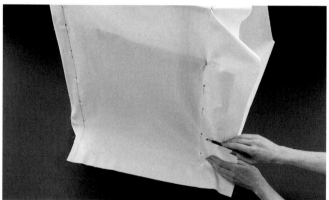

15 Pin the side pattern to the front pattern, vertically from dots to the floor. Mark seamline. Pin and mark vertical seamline between dots. Trim to within 1" (2.5 cm) of the marked seamline on side and front pieces.

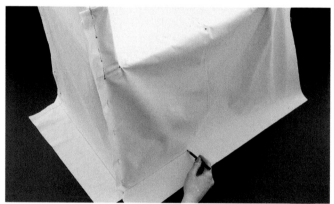

16 Mark the finished length around lower edge, where patterns reach the floor.

17 Remove the pins that hold pattern pieces to chair. Check to see that all seamlines and intersecting dots are marked and match. Remove pattern from chair. Remove pins from pattern pieces.

18 Straighten all the seamlines, using a straightedge. Add ½" (1.3 cm) seam allowances to seams as indicated by red lines. Add 2" (5 cm) hem allowance to lower edges. Fold the back and front pattern pieces in half along center lines. Cut out patterns on the cutting lines.

HOW TO SEW THE SLIPCOVER

1 Lay out and cut slipcover pieces; turn over the side pattern when cutting the slipcover piece for the opposite side. Transfer all dots from pattern to slipcover.

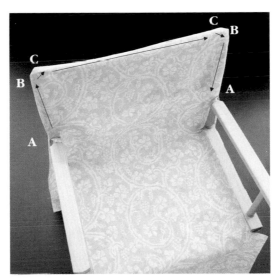

2 Pin front and back pieces, right sides together, along upper edge and back posts, matching Dots A, B, and C. Stitch ½" (1.3 cm) seam, starting and ending at Dots A and pivoting at Dots B and C; clip to dots as necessary. Press the seam open; finish seam. Turn right side out.

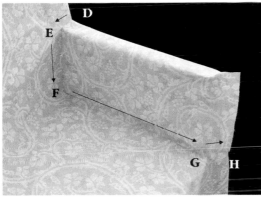

3 Pin side piece to front piece, matching dots; clip to dots as necessary. Stitch ½" (1.3 cm) seam from Dots D to H as indicated, pivoting at corners. Repeat for opposite side. Press seams open; finish seams.

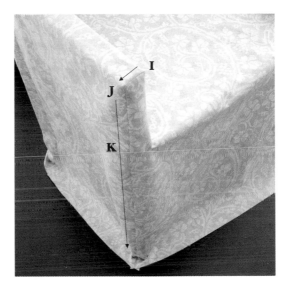

4 Pin the front arm of the side piece, right sides together, matching Dots I and J at the upper front arm and Dots K at the lower outer arm. Stitch ½" (1.3 cm) seam from Dots I to J; pivot at Dot J and continue stitching through Dot K to lower edge of slipcover. Repeat for opposite side. Press seams open; finish seams.

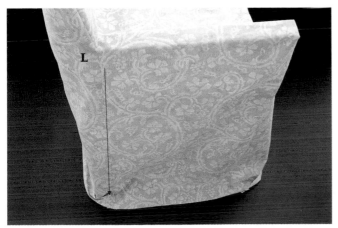

5 Stitch ½" (1.3 cm) seam from Dot L at upper outer arm to the lower edge of slipcover. Repeat for the opposite side. Press seams open; finish seams.

6 Press under 1" (2.5 cm) twice to wrong side, at the lower edge of the slipcover; stitch to make double-fold hem. Place the slipcover on the chair. Make a mock box pillow (page 123), 2" to 3" (5 to 7.5 cm) high, to fit the chair seat.

Accessories

PRESSING FLOWERS

Pressed flowers make beautiful accents for many home decorating accessories, including floral sun catchers, botanical artwork, and overdipped candles (pages 100 to 109). The pressed flowers are inexpensive to make, using flowers from your garden and a handmade flower press.

THE FLOWER PRESS

Although you have probably pressed flowers between the pages of a heavy book, a flower press will produce better results. The flower press consists of wooden front and back covers, with layers of corrugated cardboard between them. The flowers are pressed between the cardboard layers, with blotter paper or blank newsprint on both sides of the flowers. The blotter paper or newsprint absorbs the moisture from the flowers. The wing nuts on the corners of the press are tightened, to flatten the flowers as they dry.

FLOWER SELECTION

Flowers dried in a flower press usually retain much of their original color and take on a translucent quality. Select flowers that are in perfect condition, dry, and free of insects. Almost any flower can be preserved in a press, but some work better than others. Flat flowers and flowers with only a few petals, such as pansies and violas, can be pressed intact and, when pressed, will retain their natural form. However, to press flowers with thick, hard centers, you must take the flowers apart, petal by petal, because of the difference in thickness between the flower parts. Then reassemble the flowers, gluing the petals together, when you use them in a project. The thick, hard centers must be pressed in a different layer of the flower press from the petals. Or discard the centers and substitute similar, but flatter, centers from another variety when reassembling the flowers.

Bell-shaped flowers, which are difficult to take apart, generally look better as three-dimensional, rather than pressed, flowers. Rose petals press well, but they cannot be reassembled into the original shape of the rose. Rosebuds can be sliced in half with a razor blade, and then pressed.

PRESSING THE FLOWERS

The flowers must remain in the press until they have lost all their moisture and feel papery. This usually takes one to two weeks, depending on the thickness of the flowers and the amount of moisture in the flowers at the time they were put into the flower press. Changing the sheets of blotter paper or the newsprint after several days speeds the process and prevents the flowers from mildewing and

browning; however, you risk damaging the flower when it is transferred to the fresh paper. To remove the flowers from the press, either when changing the paper or when the flowers are completely dry, use tweezers with flat, rounded ends, such as those designed for stamp collecting. The sheets of blotter paper or newsprint can be reused after they have dried, provided they are not stained with mildew or dyes from the flowers.

Keep a log, listing the types of flowers that are being pressed in each layer, the dates they were put into the press, and the dates the blotter paper was changed. You may also want to include other information, such as where the flowers were gathered. By keeping a record, you will know exactly what is in the press without disturbing the materials before they are dry.

MATERIALS

- Two pieces of ½" (1.3 cm) plywood or medium-density fiberboard (MDF), each 9¾" × 12¼" (25 × 31.2 cm).

- Four ¼" × 3½" (6 mm × 9 cm) bolts with wing nuts and washers.

- Several sheets of corrugated cardboard with smooth, flat surfaces on both sides, each 9½" × 12" (24.3 × 30.5 cm).

- Several sheets of 19" × 24" (48.5 × 61 cm) blotter paper, each cut into four pieces that measure 9½" × 12" (24.3 × 30.5 cm); blank newsprint may be substituted, but do not use paper toweling or other textured papers that could imprint the flowers.

- Adhesive tabs, for numbering the cardboard layers.

- Mat knife; 220-grit sandpaper; drill and ¼" drill bit.

- Tweezers with flat, rounded ends, such as tweezers used by stamp collectors, for removing pressed flowers.

- Small notebook, for recording data.

- Plastic sleeves, wax paper, or wax paper envelopes used by stamp collectors, for storing the pressed flowers.

HOW TO MAKE A FLOWER PRESS

1 Measure ¾" (2 cm) from edges at each corner of wooden top cover; mark. Drill holes in the cover, using ¼" drill bit.

2 Use top cover as guide for marking position of holes in bottom cover. Drill holes in bottom cover. Sand all edges and surfaces of the covers.

3 Stain or paint covers, if desired. Decorate the top cover, if desired, gluing dried floral materials or other embellishments in place.

4 Measure and mark the sides of the cardboard 2" (5 cm) from each corner. Using straightedge, draw a diagonal line across each corner, connecting the marks. Trim off each corner, using a mat knife.

5 Repeat step 4 for all pieces of cardboard and for the sheets of blotter paper or newsprint. Attach adhesive tabs to the edges of the cardboard pieces, labeling each of the layers consecutively.

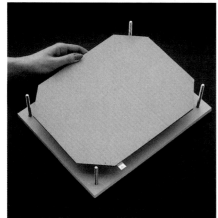

6 Assemble the press by putting the bolts through the back cover, from outside to inside. Lay the back cover on a flat surface, with inside facing up. Center the first sheet of cardboard over the cover.

7 Stack two sheets of blotter paper or four sheets of newsprint on top of the cardboard. Repeat the layers of cardboard and paper, ending with a piece of cardboard.

8 Insert the bolts through top cover. Place washers over the bolts, and secure with wing nuts.

HOW TO PRESS FLOWERS

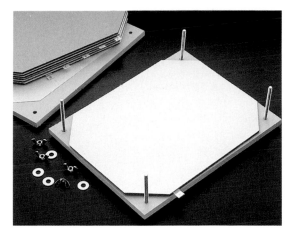

1 Remove top cover of the press, and remove all layers except the first piece of cardboard and one sheet of blotter paper or two sheets of newsprint.

2 Cut the stems close to flowers. Arrange the floral materials to be pressed on blotter paper or newsprint, allowing 1" (2.5 cm) of space around each item. Press materials of the same thickness on each layer.

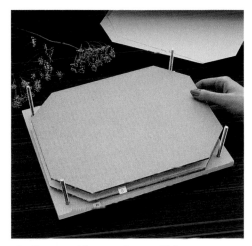

3 Cover with one sheet of blotter paper or two sheets of newsprint; then cover with one piece of cardboard.

4 Repeat steps 2 and 3 for any additional layers, sandwiching floral materials between the blotter paper or newsprint and separating each of the layers with cardboard. Keep a record of the items being pressed on each layer, along with the date they were put into the press and where they were gathered.

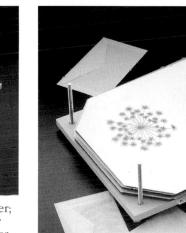

5 Insert bolts into corners of top cover; place a washer and a wing nut over the bolt at each corner. Secure the cover, tightening wing nuts as far as possible. Retighten wing nuts every day until they are fully tightened.

6 Check floral materials after one to two weeks to see if they are completely dry; take care not to disturb other layers. When dry, remove floral materials carefully, using tweezers, and store them flat in plastic sleeves, between layers of wax paper, or in wax paper envelopes. Label contents. Store the pressed flowers away from light and humidity.

PRESSED-FLOWER SUN CATCHERS

Sun catchers reflect sunlight from a window, casting prismatic light on surfaces in the room. The paper-thin pressed flowers in these sun catchers are translucent and brilliant in color.

Make the pressed flowers as on pages 96 to 99, using flowers from your garden. Then encase the flowers between a layer of precut beveled glass and a layer of extra-thin glass cut to size using a glass cutter. The outer edges of the sun catcher are sealed with copper foil tape.

SPECIALTY SUPPLIES & TECHNIQUES

The supplies needed for sun catchers are available at any stained glass supply store. The precut glass bevels come in assorted sizes and shapes. Bevels with straight sides work best, because the foil tape does not wrap smoothly around the edge of a curve. Purchase a little more of the extra-thin glass than your project requires. It is quite inexpensive, and you will want to experiment with the cutting process. Also keep in mind that there may be some breakage. To keep breakage to a minimum, use light pressure when you score the glass, especially at the edges, and keep the wheel of the glass cutter lubricated with a light oil. Use safety glasses when you are cutting glass, to guard your eyes from flying glass chips. When cleaning up, use a hand broom, not your hand, to sweep the work surface.

- Beveled glass square, rectangle, or triangle in desired size.
- Pressed flowers, leaves, and grasses as desired.
- Extra-thin glass; glass cutter; grozing pliers.
- 24-gauge copper wire; ⅜" (1 cm) copper foil tape.
- Fine-tip marking pen; cork-backed straightedge; masking tape.

HOW TO CUT THE GLASS

1 Trace the shape of beveled glass piece onto extra-thin glass, using fine-tip marking pen. Use outer edges of the glass sheet as one or two sides whenever possible.

2 Place a straightedge along one marked line on the glass, from one edge of the glass sheet completely across to the opposite edge. Check to see that the wheel of the glass cutter (arrow) will line up exactly on the marked line.

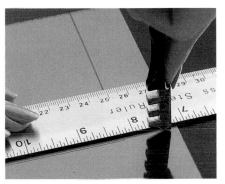

3 Hold the glass cutter perpendicular to the glass, with the wheel parallel to straightedge, beginning ⅛" (3 mm) from one edge of the glass. Hold the straightedge firmly in place with other hand.

4 Push or pull glass cutter, depending on which feels more comfortable for you, across the glass, from edge to edge, to score the glass; exert firm pressure, maintain a constant speed, and keep the glass cutter perpendicular to the glass. Ease up on the pressure as you score off the edges of the glass on the opposite side. Score the glass only once; do not repeat the process.

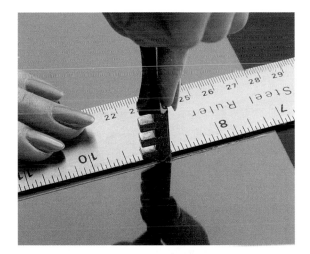

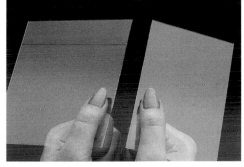

5 Hold the glass in both hands, with the scored line between your thumbs; curl your fingers under the glass, making fists, with knuckles touching each other.

6 Apply quick, even pressure as you roll your thumbs out from each other, turning your wrists upward; this breaks the glass along the scored line.

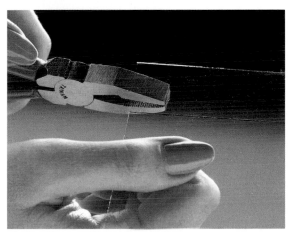

7 Repeat steps 2 to 6 for each of the remaining lines marked on the glass. For pieces that are too narrow to grasp with your fingers, use grozing pliers for safety and to obtain more leverage; hold the pliers at a right angle close to the end of the score and with flat jaw of the pliers on top of glass.

HOW TO MAKE A PRESSED-FLOWER SUN CATCHER
WITH A CORNER HANGER

1 Cut extra-thin glass (page 101) to the size of the beveled glass. Clean both surfaces of the beveled glass and the extra-thin glass piece with glass cleaner and lint-free cloth or paper towel.

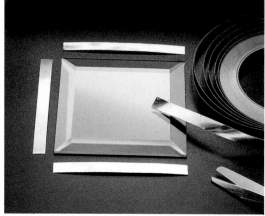

2 Cut a length of the foil tape to the exact measurement of each side of beveled glass.

3 Place extra-thin glass piece facedown on clean surface. Arrange pressed flowers and leaves on center of glass in an area not larger than the center portion of beveled glass; materials under the bevel would appear distorted.

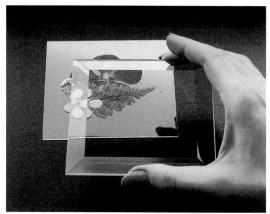

4 Place beveled glass, flat side down, over the pressed flowers, aligning glass edges. Adjust flower placement, if necessary.

5 Apply small pieces of masking tape to all sides of the sun catcher to hold it firmly together, keeping the flowers in place.

6 Decide which corner will contain hanger. Make hanger by forming a loop in copper wire, and cut the wire ends so they extend at least halfway down each adjacent side.

7 Peel paper backing from the strip of foil tape for lower edge of sun catcher. Holding the layered pieces of glass firmly in one hand, apply the foil tape to lower edge, centering tape on outer edge of glass so equal amounts will wrap to front and back.

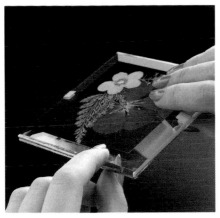

8 Fold the foil tape to the front and back, smoothing it in place.

9 Apply foil tape to any remaining sides of the sun catcher that will not contain the hanger wire.

10 Apply tape to the sides adjacent to upper corner of sun catcher, centering the hanger wire along the edges of the glass and encasing it under the strips of foil tape.

11 Smooth all sides of the foil tape firmly, using handle of wooden spoon or wooden craft stick to ease out any bubbles or gaps.

12 Suspend sun catcher in a window, using fine nylon thread. For greater impact, arrange several sun catchers in one window.

HOW TO MAKE A PRESSED-FLOWER SUN CATCHER WITH THE HANGER CENTERED ON ONE SIDE

1 Follow steps 1 to 5, opposite. Decide which side will contain hanger. Make hanger by forming a loop in copper wire, and cut the wire ends so they extend to outer corners of the side.

2 Follow steps 7 to 9, opposite. Before removing paper backing from foil tape for upper side of sun catcher, cut small slit in center of foil tape, just large enough to insert the loop of the hanger.

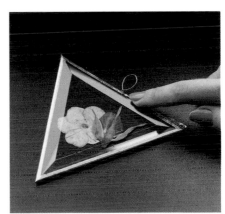

3 Apply the tape to the upper side, centering wire along the edge of glass and encasing it under the tape. Complete sun catcher as in steps 11 and 12, above.

FRAMED BOTANICALS

Pressed flowers and leaves can be mounted in prematted frames for a classic wall arrangement. The natural beauty of pressed flowers surpasses that of botanical prints, at a fraction of the cost.

Single large leaves or clusters of small pressed flowers and grasses can be arranged on rice paper for a textural background. Then cover the botanical materials with a sheet of extra-thin glass to hold them securely, and place the layers in a purchased frame.

MATERIALS

- Inexpensive frame with a precut mat.
- Extra-thin glass.
- Glass cutter.
- Rice paper.

- Pressed flowers, leaves, or grasses (page 96).
- Double-stick framer's tape or craft glue.
- Brads; split-joint pliers.

HOW TO MAKE FRAMED BOTANICALS

1 Remove the backing, precut mat, and glass from frame. Cut a piece of extra-thin glass, as on page 101, cutting it to same size as the glass provided with the frame. Clean both of the glass pieces thoroughly.

2 Cut rice paper to fit the backing provided with frame. Attach paper to backing at corners, using double-stick framer's tape or dots of glue.

3 Arrange pressed floral materials on the rice paper, checking to see that arrangement fits within mat opening.

4 Position extra-thin glass over pressed floral materials and rice paper. Position precut mat over extra-thin glass.

5 Position the original glass over precut mat and other layers; then position the frame over the glass.

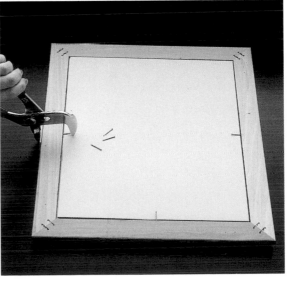

6 Turn frame over, keeping all layers firmly in place. Secure the layers into the frame, using small brads and split-joint pliers; pressure between layers keeps the flowers in place.

DECORATIVE CANDLES

Candles add instant charm to any room and, when lit, create a comforting atmosphere and a feeling of warmth. But, because purchased decorative candles are usually expensive, some people hesitate to burn them. Rather than buy decorative candles, you can make your own, inexpensively.

Overdipped candles (opposite and left) are embellished with pressed flowers and leaves, charms, and narrow strips of paper as on pages 108 and 109.

Rolled beeswax candles (above and right) are easily made from pure beeswax sheets as on pages 109 to 113. Various shapes can be made. Above are a cone-shaped candle (left), basic tapers (center), a tall round pillar (right), and a short square pillar (front). At right are several spiral tapers: an unfluted one-color spiral (near right), a fluted two-color spiral (center), and a fluted one-color spiral (far right).

OVERDIPPED CANDLES

Pressed flowers, narrow strips of decorative paper, and other thin materials can be added to the surface of a candle; then the candle is overdipped to seal the materials with a light coating of wax. In this way, inexpensive plain candles can become one-of-a-kind candles that would cost far more in a specialty shop.

The floating-wax method of overdipping works well to eliminate the need for a large quantity of wax. A metal container is first filled with hot water. Melted wax is then poured over the water and floats on the surface. As the candle is dipped down into the water and up through the wax, the floating wax clings to the candle. Because the water is not as hot as the wax, it does not affect the surface of the candle.

The wax should be melted slowly over indirect heat, using a double boiler. Or use a metal container set into a larger pan of water, with a metal rack placed in the water pan to raise the upper container. The wax can be melted on a stovetop or on a hot plate. A candy thermometer is used to check the temperature of the melted wax. Avoid pouring any water that may contain melted wax into the sink, because wax solidifies quickly and would clog the drain.

HOW TO DECORATE A CANDLE FOR OVERDIPPING

MATERIALS

- Candle in desired shape and size; for best results, a colored candle should have a solid color, not an overdipped color.
- Pressed flowers (page 96), lightweight papers, or other thin materials, for decorating the candle.
- Stainless steel spoon.
- Hot plate or stovetop burner.
- Soft work surface, such as a surface covered with several layers of fabric.
- Double boiler or alternative cans or saucepans.
- Paraffin wax.
- Freezer paper.
- Pliers; candy thermometer.

1 Place the bowl of a spoon over stovetop burner or hot plate, heated to low setting; or lean the bowl of a spoon against the soleplate of an iron at low setting. Arrange the pressed flowers or other thin materials as desired on the work surface to determine design you want to follow.

2 Transfer one of the larger items to surface of the candle. Roll the heated bowl of the spoon over the surface of the item, working from center to outer edges and melting the wax under it; continue until all areas of the item are held in place by the rehardened wax. Reheat the spoon as needed.

3 Position and affix other items in the same manner, working with larger items first and filling in the spaces as desired with smaller items. Overdip the candle to seal the pressed-flower design to the candle surface, using the floating-wax method (opposite).

HOW TO OVERDIP A CANDLE
USING THE FLOATING-WAX METHOD

1 Place about ½ lb. (250 g) of wax in top of double boiler; place over a pan of hot water, and heat the wax to 205°F (96°C). Heat the water in a tall can to just below boiling; remove from heat. Slowly pour the wax onto surface of hot water, taking care not to cause bubbles to form in the wax. Remove any bubbles with a wooden spoon.

2 Hold candle by the wick with pliers. Dip candle up to wick; remove from dipping can. Allow to cool for a few seconds. Repeat the dipping process. Stand the candle on freezer paper to cool; or, if overdipping a candle that will not stand alone, clamp the wick securely and hang candle until cool.

ROLLED BEESWAX CANDLES

Honeycomb beeswax candles can be made by rolling sheets of pure beeswax around a length of candle wicking. By cutting the sheets to different sizes and, sometimes, at an angle, you can make a variety of candle styles. To cut the sheets, use a straightedge and a rotary cutter, such as a pizza cutter, or a sharp knife. For ease in rolling the candles, work with beeswax sheets that are at room temperature.

The sheets and the candle wicking can be purchased inexpensively from craft stores and mail-order suppliers. Beeswax sheets are available in many decorating colors

in addition to the natural honey color. Beeswax is smokeless and long burning. Each sheet of beeswax burns about eight hours. Occasionally beeswax develops a frosty or dusty appearance called *bloom*. This harmless characteristic can be removed by simply passing a hair dryer lightly over the the candle or by setting it in a warm place for a short time.

The correct wick size is important, to allow the candle to burn for the longest possible time, without smoking or dripping, or extinguishing itself. For candles up to 3" (7.5 cm) in diameter, use a 2/0 wick size.

HOW TO MAKE A ROLLED BEESWAX CANDLE

MATERIALS

- Beeswax sheet or sheets, 8½" × 16¾" (21.8 × 42.4 cm) in size.
- 2/0 candle wicking.
- Rotary cutter, such as pizza cutter, or sharp knife.
- Ruler or yardstick, to be used as a straightedge and for measuring.
- Metal pie plate, optional.

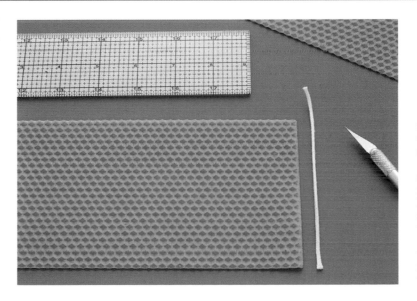

1 Cut sheet or sheets of beeswax as necessary to obtain desired candle size and shape (pages 111 to 113); use a straightedge and rotary cutter or sharp knife, for smooth, straight cuts. Cut the candle wicking 1" (2.5 cm) longer than the desired finished length of the candle.

(Continued)

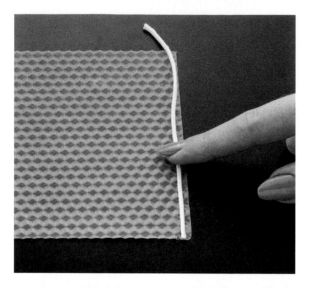

2 Place wick about ⅛" (3 mm) from the side of beeswax sheet that will run the length of candle; position wick even with lower edge of sheet, extending it 1" (2.5 cm) beyond upper edge. Press wick firmly into wax.

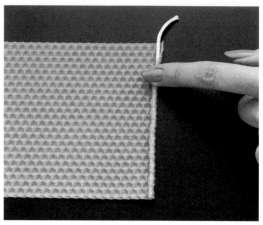

3 Roll edge of sheet over wick; press firmly, embedding wick in beeswax. The first roll of wax around wick should be tight and even.

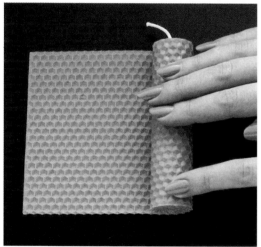

4 Roll beeswax sheet, keeping even pressure along the length of the candle. Keep lower edge straight for a flat candle base.

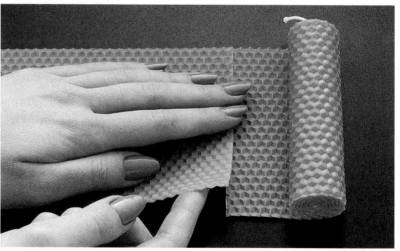

5 Join additional sheet or partial sheet, if needed for larger candle, by lapping new sheet over previous sheet for ⅛" (3 mm); press edge firmly to affix the new sheet. Continue rolling until all pieces are joined and rolled.

6 Seal outer edge of last sheet to outside of candle by pressing firmly along edge.

7 Heat a metal pie plate on stovetop burner. Place bottom of the candle on the heated pie plate; this melts the wax on the bottom, leveling the candle and sealing the wick. If candle is level, this step may be omitted.

BASIC TAPERS

A pair of basic tapers, about ½" × 8" (1.3 × 20.5 cm), is made from one beeswax sheet.

1 Cut the sheet in half. Make an angled cut across upper long end of one half, from the corner at one side to a point ¾" (2 cm) from corner on opposite side. Place wick on the longest edge, as in step 2, opposite.

2 Roll the candles as in steps 3 and 4, keeping the lower edge even; complete the candles as in steps 6 and 7.

SPIRAL TAPERS

A pair of spiral tapers, 16" (40.5 cm) tall, is made from one beeswax sheet.

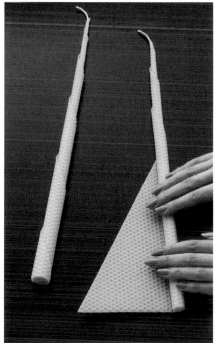

1 **Unfluted tapers.** Cut sheet in half on the diagonal; one triangular piece is used for each taper.

2 Place wick on long straight edge of triangular piece, as in step 2, opposite. Roll the candles as in steps 3 and 4, keeping lower edges even; complete candles as in steps 6 and 7.

Fluted tapers. Follow steps 1 and 2 for unfluted tapers, left. Flare diagonal edges of tapers by holding the beeswax between the thumb and forefinger and pulling out gently.

TWO-COLOR SPIRAL TAPERS

A pair of two-color spiral tapers, 16" (40.5 cm) tall, is made from one beeswax sheet of each color.

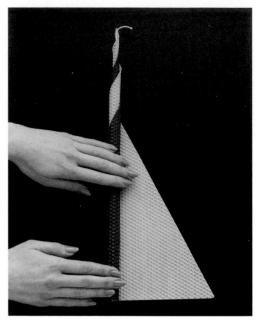

1 Cut both beeswax sheets in half on the diagonal. Set aside one triangular piece of each color.

2 Cut 1" (2.5 cm) from lower edge of one triangular piece.

3 Place shorter triangular piece on table; place taller triangular piece of second color on top, aligning lower edges. Complete candle as for spiral taper on page 111, step 2. Flute edges of the tapers as on page 111, if desired. Make another taper, using remaining triangular piece of each color.

CONE-SHAPED CANDLE

Cone-shaped candle, 8" (20.5 cm) tall, is made from two beeswax sheets.

1 Make an angled cut across long side of beeswax sheet, from corner at one side to a point 2¼" (6 cm) from corner on opposite side. These pieces are referred to as Pieces A and D as indicated.

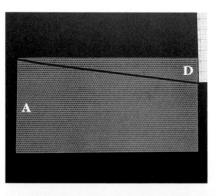

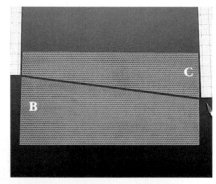

2 Make an angled cut across long side of the second beeswax sheet, from a point 2¼" (6 cm) from corner at one side to a point 4¼" (10.8 cm) from the corner on the opposite side. These pieces are referred to as Pieces B and C.

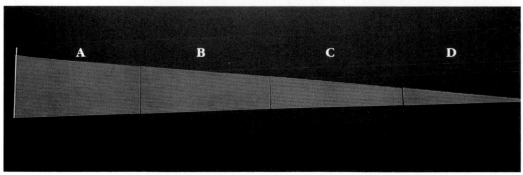

3 Position Pieces A, B, C, and D so sides of pieces align as shown; upper edges of pieces are angled, and lower edges are straight. Make candle as on page 110, steps 2 to 7, placing wick on edge of Piece A as shown and rolling candle from longest edge to tapered point.

PILLAR CANDLES

Pillar candle, about 2" × 4" (5 × 10 cm) is made from one beeswax sheet. A tall pillar, about 2½" × 8" (6.5 × 20.5 cm), is made from four sheets.

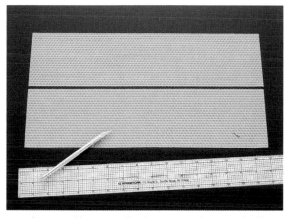

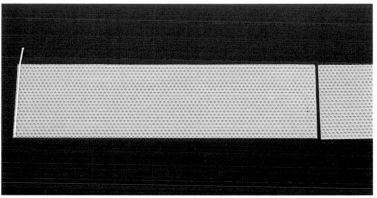

1 **Short pillar.** Cut the beeswax sheet in half lengthwise.

2 Place half-sheets end to end. Make the candle as on page 110, steps 2 to 7, placing wick on one short edge. If a wider candle is desired, up to 3" (7.5 cm) in diameter, add more half-sheets.

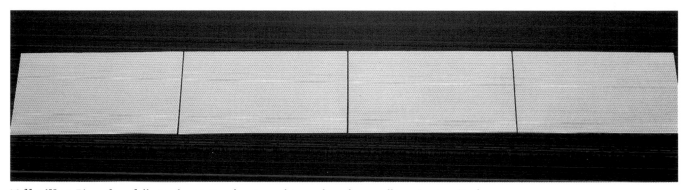

Tall pillar. Place four full-size beeswax sheets end to end; make candle as in step 2, above.

SQUARED PILLAR

Squared pillar candle, about 2" × 4" (5 × 10 cm) is made from one beeswax sheet. Four sheets are used for a 2½" × 8" (6.5 × 20.5 cm) squared pillar.

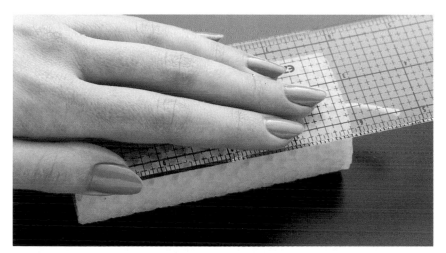

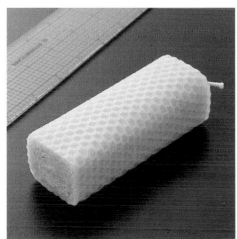

1 Make short or tall pillar candle, above. Place candle on table, and place straightedge on top; press down on straightedge to flatten candle.

2 Turn candle one quarter turn; flatten remaining sides.

DECORATIVE BOXES

Decorative boxes grouped on a table can add interest to a room and cost very little. Small, sturdy, cardboard boxes you have on hand and inexpensive cardboard boxes purchased at a craft store can be wrapped with interesting papers for a novelty look.

For simplicity in covering the boxes, choose boxes that have attached, hinged lids. Or, if you have boxes with separate lids, convert them to hinged lids by attaching the lids as shown below.

Select inexpensive or recycled papers, such as old sheet music, maps, or newspapers. Create eye-catching collages for the lids from found items, such as trinkets, pieces of corrugated cardboard, torn papers, and old buttons.

MATERIALS

- Sturdy cardboard box with attached lid, or box with separate lid converted to attached lid; corrugated cardboard box is not suitable.
- Inexpensive or recycled paper, such as old sheet music, maps, or newspapers.
- Vinyl tape, 1" (2.5 cm) wide, for making a hinged lid.
- Thick craft glue.
- Sponge applicator.
- Miscellaneous found items, for lid embellishments.
- Ribbon or small tassel, for optional lid tab.
- Ruler; mat knife; scissors.

HOW TO MAKE A HINGED LID ON A BOX

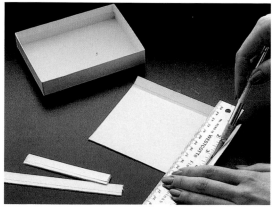

1 Remove the sides from the lid of the box, using mat knife.

2 Place lid piece on top of box, with back edges even. Secure it with vinyl tape along the back edge, keeping lid in closed position.

HOW TO MAKE A DECORATIVE BOX

1 Measure the box accurately from one back edge, around the sides and front, to the opposite back edge. Draw a rectangle on back side of paper to be used for covering the box, with length of rectangle equal to this measurement; width of rectangle is equal to height of box. If paper is not large enough, sheets may be pieced together by overlapping the edges and gluing them together.

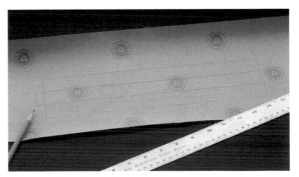

2 Draw ½" (1.3 cm) extensions on each side. Draw 1" (2.5 cm) extension on upper edge, excluding the side extensions. Draw 1" (2.5 cm) extension for lower edge, including side extensions. Cut paper on marked lines.

(Continued)

3 Apply craft glue to the back side of paper, using sponge applicator; dilute glue with water, if necessary, just enough to spread easily.

4 Affix paper to front and sides of the box, wrapping the ½" (1.3 cm) extensions around to the back of box and allowing 1" (2.5 cm) to extend at top and bottom.

5 Clip upper edge of paper at each front corner. Smooth extension to inside of box on the front and sides, overlapping the paper at the corners as necessary.

6 Wrap extension onto the bottom of the box, mitering corners. Secure miters with glue.

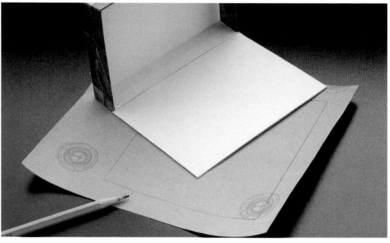

7 Open the lid. Trace lid and back of box onto paper, marking the points where lid is attached.

8 Add ½" (1.3 cm) extensions to the front and sides of lid portion. Add ½" (1.3 cm) extension to lower back edge. Cut out paper.

9 Apply glue to back side of paper; affix it to lid and back of box, wrapping extensions to underside of lid and mitering the corners. Close lid. Wrap extension at lower back edge onto the bottom of the box.

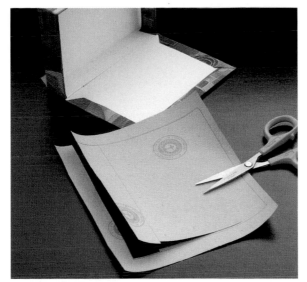

10 Trace lid onto paper, for the lid lining. Add 1" (2.5 cm) extension on the back edge. Cut out paper, cutting ⅛" (3 mm) inside the marked lines on the front and side edges.

11 Glue a folded 3" (7.5 cm) length of ribbon or a small tassel to bottom of lid at center front, to form tab for lifting lid.

12 Apply glue to lid lining piece; affix it to bottom of lid. Smooth extension at back edge of lid to inside back of box.

13 Trace bottom of box onto paper. Cut out the paper, cutting ⅛" (3 mm) inside the marked lines. Apply glue; affix to outside of box bottom.

15 Embellish the lid with found items, arranging items as desired.

14 Close lid; secure with rubber bands or weight down the lid until glue is completely dry.

RAG RUG PILLOWS

Inexpensive rag rugs can be easily transformed into decorator pillows with appealing texture. Made from large rugs, these pillows can be used as comfortable floor pillows, providing additional seating in a family room; from small rugs, they make accent pillows for the sofa.

Because the finished size of a rag rug pillow depends on the size of the rug, you may not be able to use a purchased pillow form. If a purchased pillow form is not available in the size you need, make your own form by stitching together two layers of polyester upholstery batting and stuffing polyester fiberfill between the layers. Or, in some cases, you may find a bed pillow that fits.

MATERIALS

- Woven rag rug.
- Heavy-duty thread, such as pearl cotton or button and carpet thread; large-eyed needle.

- Purchased pillow form in desired size; or polyester upholstery batting and polyester fiberfill, to make a pillow form.

HOW TO MAKE A PILLOW FORM

1 Cut two pieces of polyester upholstery batting to the desired finished size of the pillow. Thread a large-eyed needle with a double strand of heavy thread; knot end.

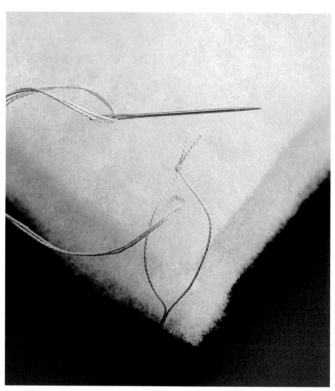

2 Layer the two pieces of batting. At one corner, run the needle through both layers and then between the threads, above the knot. Pull tight.

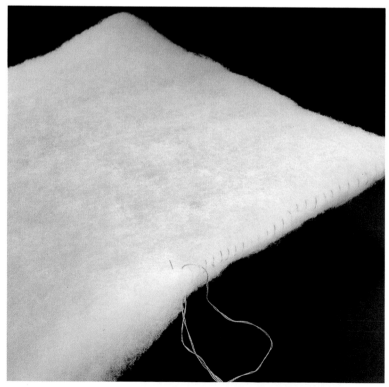

3 Whipstitch the layers together along three sides as shown. Knot thread securely each time you run out of thread, and begin again by securing the thread as in step 2.

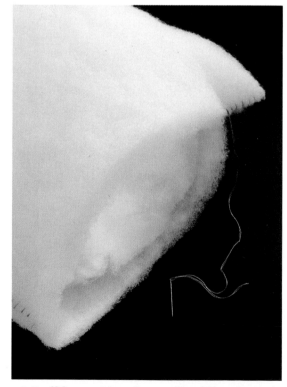

4 Stuff form with polyester fiberfill to desired fullness. Whipstitch the last side closed. Knot thread securely.

1 Fold the rag rug in half, aligning the fringed ends; pin. Thread a large-eyed needle with a double strand of heavy thread. Stitch fringed ends of rug together, taking ¼" (6 mm) stitches.

2 Refold the stitched rug so the fringe is about one-third the distance from the top fold. Turn fringe toward the bottom fold.

4 Insert pillow form (opposite). Stitch the open side closed, folding top and bottom of rug at marked points. Knot securely.

3 Stitch folded rug together along one side, using a double strand of heavy thread. Mark opposite side of rug at top and bottom folds.

MOCK BOX PILLOWS

Mock box pillows are easy to make, with pleated corners that are simply folded in place. Suitable for any decorating style, the pillows may be plain or trimmed with welting. Large pillows can be stacked for use as floor pillows, or smaller ones used as accent pillows. A mock box pillow can also serve as the cushion for a twig ottoman (page 71).

Pillow forms are available in many sizes, up to 30" (76 cm) square. They vary in price, depending on the amount and type of filling used and on the quality of the cover fabric. For economy, you can use pillow forms filled with polyester fiberfill; the down pillow forms are more expensive.

If desired, you can make your own pillow forms inexpensively by stitching together two layers of polyester upholstery batting and stuffing polyester fiberfill between the layers of batting. By making your own pillow forms, you are able to create them in dimensions that may not be available ready-made.

MATERIALS

- Fabric, for pillow front and back.
- Contrasting fabric and cording, for optional welting.
- Purchased pillow form, or polyester upholstery batting and polyester fiberfill if you are making the pillow form. The length of the form is equal to the combined measurement of the desired length and thickness of the finished pillow; the width of the form is equal to the combined measurement of the desired width and thickness of the finished pillow.

CUTTING DIRECTIONS

For the pillow front and pillow back, cut two pieces of fabric, 1" (2.5 cm) longer than the desired finished length of the pillow plus the desired finished thickness, or loft, of the pillow. The cut width of the pillow front and pillow back is 1" (2.5 cm) wider than the desired finished width of the pillow plus the desired finished thickness.

If you are making the pillow form, cut two batting pieces, with the length of the pieces equal to the desired finished length of the pillow plus the desired finished thickness, or loft, of the pillow. The cut width of the batting pieces is equal to the desired finished width of the pillow plus the desired finished thickness.

If welting is desired, cut fabric strips on the bias; for economical use of fabric, the strips may be cut at an angle less than 45°. To determine how wide to cut the strips, wrap a piece of fabric around the cording, pinning it together. Measure this distance, and add 1" (2.5 cm) for seam allowances. Cut the bias fabric strips for the welting to this width; the combined length of the fabric strips is equal to the distance around the pillow plus extra for seam allowances.

HOW TO MAKE A MOCK BOX PILLOW

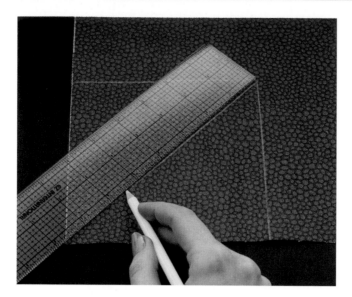

1 Mark a square on the right side of the fabric at one corner, using chalk, with each side of the square measuring one-half of the desired thickness of the finished pillow plus ½" (1.3 cm). Draw a diagonal line through square, ending at corner of fabric.

2 Fold fabric on the marked lines of the square, bringing the folds to the diagonal line. Pin in place.

3 Baste across the pleats within the ½" (1.3 cm) seam allowance. Trim off triangular section of excess fabric at the corner.

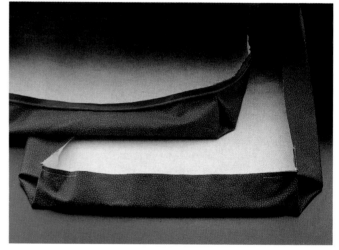

4 Repeat steps 1 to 3 for all corners of pillow front and pillow back. If welting is desired, make and apply the welting, as in steps 1 to 5, opposite.

5 Pin the pillow front to the pillow back, right sides together, matching corner tucks. Stitch around pillow in ½" (1.3 cm) seam, leaving an opening on one side for turning. If pillow has welting, use a zipper foot and stitch inside previous stitching line, crowding stitches against the welting.

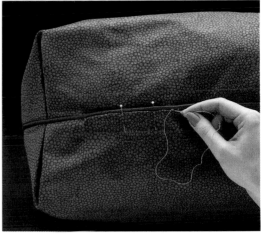

6 Turn the pillow right side out through opening. Use purchased pillow form, or make pillow form as on page 120, steps 1 to 4. Punch in corners of the pillow form, and insert it into mock box pillow cover.

7 Slipstitch the opening closed.

HOW TO MAKE & APPLY THE WELTING

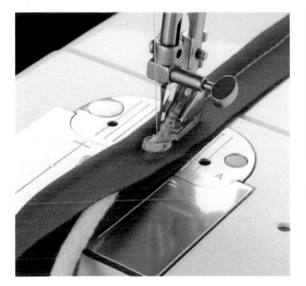

1 Cut the fabric strips (page 123); seam the strips together as necessary for the desired length. Fold the fabric strip around the cording, wrong sides together, matching raw edges. Using a zipper foot, machine-baste close to cording; smooth cording as you stitch, removing twists.

2 Stitch welting to right side of fabric, over previous stitches, matching raw edges and starting 2" (5 cm) from the end of the welting; clip and ease welting at corners.

3 Stop stitching 2" (5 cm) from the point where ends of welting will meet. Cut off one end of welting so it overlaps the other end by 1" (2.5 cm).

4 Remove the stitching from one end of the welting, and trim ends of the cording so they just meet.

5 Fold under ½" (1.3 cm) of fabric on overlapping end of welting. Lap it around the other end; finish stitching welting to pillow front.

CREDITS

CY DECOSSE INCORPORATED

Chairman/CEO: Philip L. Penny
Chairman Emeritus: Cy DeCosse
President/COO: Nino Tarantino
Executive V.P./Editor-in-Chief:
  William B. Jones

AFFORDABLE DECORATING
Created by: The Editors of
  Cy DeCosse Incorporated

Also available from the publisher:
*Bedroom Decorating, Creative Window
Treatments, Decorating for Christmas,
Decorating the Living Room, Creative
Accessories for the Home, Decorating
with Silk & Dried Flowers, Decorating
the Kitchen, Decorative Painting,
Decorating Your Home for Christmas,
Decorating for Dining & Entertaining,
Decorating with Fabric & Wallcovering,
Decorating the Bathroom, Decorating
with Great Finds, Picture-Perfect Walls,
More Creative Window Treatments,
Outdoor Decor, The Gift of Christmas*

Group Executive Editor: Zoe A. Graul
Editorial Manager: Dawn M. Anderson
Senior Technical Director: Rita C. Arndt
Senior Project Manager: Kristen Olson
Assistant Project Manager: Amy Berndt
Associate Creative Director:
  Lisa Rosenthal

Art Director: Stephanie Michaud
Writer: Rita C. Arndt
Editor: Janice Cauley
Researcher/Designer: Michael Basler
Researchers: Linda Neubauer, Lori Ritter
Sample Production Manager: Carol Olson
Lead Samplemaker: Carol Pilot
Senior Technical Photo Stylist:
  Bridget Haugh
Technical Photo Stylists: Sue Jorgensen,
  Nancy Sundeen
Styling Director: Bobbette Destiche
Project Stylist: Coralie Sathre
Prop Assistant/Shopper: Margo Morris
Artisans: Arlene Dohrman, Sharon
  Ecklund, Phyllis Galbraith, Valerie Hill,
  Kristi Kuhnau, Virginia Mateen, Ginger
  Mountin, Carol Pilot, Mary Rosendahl,
  Michelle Skudlarek, Nancy Sundeen
*Vice President of Development Planning
  & Production:* Jim Bindas
Director of Photography: Mike Parker
Creative Photo Coordinator:
  Cathleen Shannon
Studio Manager: Marcia Chambers
Lead Photographer: Stuart Block
Photographers: Rebecca Hawthorne,
  Kevin Hedden, Rex Irmen, William
  Lindner, Mark Macemon, Paul Najlis,
  Chuck Nields, Mike Parker, Greg
  Wallace
Contributing Photographers: Phil Aarrestad,
  Kim Bailey, Doug Cummelin, Paul
  Englund, Brian Holman, Steve Smith
Senior Promotional Production Manager:
  Gretchen Gundersen

Desktop Publishing Specialist:
  Laurie Kristensen
Production Staff: Deborah Eagle, Kevin
  Hedden, Jeff Hickman, Jeanette Moss,
  Michelle Peterson, Mike Schauer, Greg
  Wallace, Kay Wethern
Shop Supervisor: Phil Juntti
Scenic Carpenters: Jon Hegge, Troy
  Johnson, Rob Johnstone, John Nadeau
Consultants: Jill Engelhart, Amy
  Engman, Wendy Fedie, Mary Pausch,
  Randy Young, Kirk Ziebart
Contributors: American Efird, Inc.;
  Casual Lifestyles Distribution, Inc.;
  Conso Products Company; Decart
  Inc.; Dritz Corporation; Duncan
  Enterprises; EZ International; Fabby
  Lighting; Honey Wax; HTC-Handler
  Textile Corporation; Kirsch; Offray;
  Plaid Enterprises; Putnam Company,
  Inc.; Swavelle/Mill Creek Textiles;
  Swiss-Metrosene, Inc.; Therm O Web;
  Waverly, Division of F. Schumacher &
  Company
Printed on American paper by:
  R. R. Donnelley & Sons Co.

99 98 97 96 / 5 4 3 2 1

Cy DeCosse Incorporated offers
a variety of how-to books. For
information write:
  Cy DeCosse Subscriber Books
  5900 Green Oak Drive
  Minnetonka, MN 55343